D0146459

The Entrepreneur's Guide to Advertising

Recent Titles in
The Entrepreneur's Guide

The Entrepreneur's Guide

CJ Rhoads, Series Editor

The Entrepreneur's Guide to Advertising

James R. Ogden and Scott Rarick

PRAEGER
An Imprint of ABC-CLIO, LLC

Santa Barbara, California • Denver, Colorado • Oxford, England

Copyright 2010 by James R. Ogden and Scott Rarick

Library of Congress Cataloging-in-Publication Data

Ogden, James R.
  The entrepreneur's guide to advertising / James R. Ogden and Scott Rarick.
      p. cm. — (The entrepreneur's guide)
  Includes index.
  ISBN 978-0-313-36582-9 (hard copy : alk. paper) — ISBN 978-0-313-36583-6
(ebook)
    1. Advertising—Management.   2. Marketing—Management.
3. Entrepreneurship.   4. Small business.   I. Rarick, Scott.   II. Title.
  HF5823.O3587   2010
  659.1—dc22   2009034154

ISBN: 978-0-313-36582-9
EISBN: 978-0-313-36583-6

14   13   12   11   10   1   2   3   4   5

This book is also available on the World Wide Web as an eBook.
Visit www.abc-clio.com for details.

Praeger
An Imprint of ABC-CLIO, LLC

ABC-CLIO, LLC
130 Cremona Drive, P.O. Box 1911
Santa Barbara, California 93116-1911

This book is printed on acid-free paper ∞

Manufactured in the United States of America

Contents

Acknowledgments

The development of any project is a huge challenge. When an author commits to a writing project, he must keep in mind that personal time will suffer as a result. Because of this, we wish to acknowledge all of the assistance we have received while working on this volume.

James R. Ogden: First and foremost, I want to thank my brilliant colleague and loving soul mate, Dr. Denise T. Ogden, for her inspiration and assistance. My children, David, Anne, and Kari, along with my newest daughter Kerrie and my grandson Kaleb, are always providing guidance and help. I thank them. My college students, both undergraduates and graduates, keep me cutting edge when it comes to keeping up with the field. I thank them. My mother, Mrs. Marianne Ogden, taught me how to read and write (she thinks it was my public school education). She has also taught hundreds of others as a public school teacher. Her work ethic and positive outlook on life always makes me proud. Thank you, Mom, for teaching me the real lessons in life! My mother-in-law is a saint. Her love of family and untiring work ethic would motivate the laziest person on the planet . . . it did. Thank you, Ninfa Alarid, for your inspiration.

Finally, a thank you to my colleague and dear friend, Mr. Scott Rarick. Scott still practices the art of advertising some seven days a week, 12 hours a day. He doesn't complain. He loves his work. Although overworked, Scott has added tremendous value to this project. A loving thank you to Scott's wife, Stacy, who puts up with Scott and me, and who selflessly allowed Scott (the father of two young ones) to work on this project along with me.

Thank you Kutztown University of Pennsylvania and to all of my colleagues who reviewed this work. Paco Underhill, thanks for helping me understand the value of point-of-sale research and point-of-sale advertising and promotion. Thanks to Donald (Horilla) Waligore for being a friend of over 35 years. My sister Suzanne always makes me think through her sense of humor, so she gets a nod, as do my oldest sister, Sally, and her husband Ken. They've been married for over 35 years and still look like they're in love. That's inspiration.

Thank you to all of my readers. As this is my sixth attempt at a book; my loyal readers have followed me here. Thank you.

Scott Rarick: Thank you so much to my wife, Stacy, for having the patience to endure me during this undertaking and for giving so selflessly of her own time in occupying our boys so that I could write. I owe you, big time. And thanks to my boys, Christopher and Jacob, for providing laughter and miracles on a daily basis. You are my best creation.

Many thanks to my parents, who have instilled in me the virtues needed to be successful and the will and desire to be a good person. I'll never be able to fully repay you for giving me all that you have already. And thanks to my grandfather, Casper "Pap" Meck, for providing so much wisdom and guidance throughout the years, most of which I am only now fully appreciating. Thanks to my brothers, Kevin and Greg, for always being there and for being such good friends.

A special thanks to Peter Stevenson for sharing his creative genius and providing insight and inspiration on a daily basis. A huge thank you to dear friends and family, clients and coworkers, past and present, and all of the professors I've had the pleasure of learning from at Kutztown University. You've been my motivators, confidants, research panel, and sounding board, and for that I thank you.

Last, but far from least, I owe an endless debt of gratitude to my co-author and dear friend, Dr. James "Doc" Ogden, and his wife, Denise, for believing in me and always providing opportunity and encouragement. You've made me what I am today.

Introduction

What a great time for entrepreneurs to become involved in the fast-paced business of advertising. The explosion of technology has driven many changes in the advertising industry. New metrics for advertising measurement are being developed and instituted, and more channels of media are becoming available for businesspeople to exploit in order to drive their businesses. Advertisers are scrambling to find ways to attract customers to their stores as the economy changes daily. It is important, now more than ever, for entrepreneurs to understand the concepts and executions involved in the development of a comprehensive and integrated advertising campaign.

This book provides entrepreneurs with the tools necessary to understand the somewhat complicated world of advertising. In addition to exposing the reader to the many concepts, subjects, and ideas of advertising, the authors also provide a template system for the development of a comprehensive, research-based advertising and marketing communications plan.

In the 2000s, marketers and advertisers found that all marketing mix variables have the ability to communicate to various customer bases. In addition, we found that each of the marketing mix variables had an impact not only on each other, but on the customers as well. In order to create an efficient, cost-effective method of communicating to their audiences, advertisers began to take advantage of other methods of communication available to them in the advertising environment. Advertisers began to pay more attention to the impact that each of their Integrated Marketing Communication (IMC) variables had on the targeted audiences. Advertisers also took a look at the confusion that was caused by messages that were not synergistic and integrated. The result was an integration of all communications variables into a single plan. This plan is called the IMC plan, or marketing communications (MARCOM) plan.

In the development of an IMC plan, advertisers must make sure that they have planned for all of the executions needed to reach a given target audience. This book will provide the basic concepts, vocabulary, and templates necessary to create that plan. Since "the only constant in the universe is change," entrepreneurs must take more time in the development of their IMC plans in order to make sure their investment in advertising is being spent wisely.

This book was conceived to provide a step-by-step approach that allows the reader to build their advertising knowledge base from the ground up. Basic concepts will be provided, and then those concepts will be integrated with more complex concepts and ideas which will finally be pulled together during the last few chapters of the book. Thus, the book will begin by telling the reader what we will cover, it will then cover that material, and, at the end of the book, it will tell you what has been covered and how that information and data can be used.

It helps to see an overview of the subject matter that will be covered within the book. The next few pages take a look at each of these areas.

We have had a lot of education and experience in the advertising world. Because of that, we have added some stories and experiences that we feel will help to clarify the points and subject matter that are discussed throughout the book. In each of the chapters, we point out the important material that is needed and used in the development and execution of advertising. The book is developed with an interesting framework. The entire advertising and IMC plan will follow the model of developing objectives first, creating a strategy to achieve those objectives, and then followed by a series of "tactical executions" that will be used to actually execute the advertising and IMC plan. Additionally, each of the subjects covered individually, such as advertising, public relations, sales promotion, media, research, and others will also follow the basic format of developing objectives and then moving on to strategy and tactical executions. Please keep this in mind as you read. Knowing this will make each of the subject areas a little clearer. Now, on to the book.

The book begins with an overview of the advertising industry. In chapter 1, we take a look at the concept of marketing and how advertising fits into it. As we travel around the world, when we mention that we are involved in the marketing industry, those people with whom we speak with always assume we are referring to advertising or personal selling when, in fact, we are not. It always takes some time to explain to people that marketing and advertising are two different subjects and topics. In fact, advertising and selling are just two of the tactics available to marketing communicators when faced with developing a comprehensive and efficient marketing plan. Because of this situation, the subject of marketing must first be explained and then followed by an explanation of advertising and integrated marketing communication.

In chapter 1, we begin by defining advertising. We offer a definition so that all of the readers will be on the same page as we continue our discussions and proceed to more complicated concepts and subjects. While the job of marketing is to get the product, once produced, from the point of production to the end user, the job of advertising is to provide the best possible selling message to the correct target audience at the best possible price. This definition can also fit the definition of advertising efficiencies, which is a metric for the value you can derive from your advertising and IMC programs. Chapter 1 continues by exploring the role advertising plays in a firm or organization's marketing plan. A sample marketing plan is presented, along with step-by-step instructions to the reader for using that plan to prepare his or her own advertising plan. The overall process of marketing management is also presented to showcase how advertising and marketing need to be married or integrated with each other. A marketing plan template is provided.

To make it easier on the reader, each of the chapters, beginning with chapter 1, has been summarized with bullet points for quick reference. As chapter 1 coverage closes, we move on to chapter 2 for a look at outside suppliers of advertising and other sources of help for the entrepreneur in their quest to create the perfect advertising and IMC plans.

As stated above, chapter 2 deals with outside suppliers and other sources of help for the budding entrepreneur. We have decided to cover this material early in the book in order for the reader to assemble necessary data and information that will help in the overall execution of the advertising program. In addition to listing outside suppliers, we have provided information on when and who to select in order to help create a plan.

Chapter 2 opens with an introduction and some discussion about who or what outside suppliers are. Keep in mind that, as an entrepreneur, you cannot be an expert in all areas. Thus, it is sometimes necessary to seek the help and advice of others. The first part of the chapter talks about who those others are. The chapter continues with coverage of when to utilize outside suppliers and why. One section of the chapter has been developed and provided to help with the selection of outside suppliers. As advertising professionals, we often run into individuals (especially entrepreneurs) who are looking for help and advice concerning the development of their advertising programs. We are often eager and willing to help, so long as the entrepreneur has first attempted to help herself. The more information and knowledge the entrepreneur has in regard to their business, industry, and market, the easier it is for us to provide guidance. Also, if the entrepreneur has spent some time trying to understand the concept and subject of advertising, we feel our time is not wasted in attempting to help. What does this mean? The more information and knowledge you can generate, the more successful you will be! Pay attention to the section that offers advice on when and how to select your providers.

Chapter 2 continues by listing a number of outside suppliers the authors have found useful. The list includes suppliers of financial, industry, media, and consumer data and information. The coverage provided in chapter 2 will help you to understand and develop your advertising plan. This information will be used in later chapters as we begin to execute the plan. As chapter 2 ends, we segue into the third chapter, which covers branding.

Branding is a somewhat complicated subject that has grown in prominence over the last decade. Some advertisers and marketers have dubbed the decade of the 2000s as the "decade of branding." Although there was a lot of debate and discussion over whether the branding function should be placed within the product development and management areas or in the integrated marketing communications areas, the conclusion was that it should be prominent in both. Because of the communication value of a brand, advertisers can use it as a silent salesperson when no other marketing communication is possible, such as in a consumer's home (or in their cupboard). Because of that, a company's brand becomes a valuable asset to advertisers.

As you begin to read chapter 3, you will notice that the chapter begins with a definition of the word "brand." In particular, we take a look at what a brand is and why it should be a way of thinking, rather than just a plain logo, name, trademark, or servicemark. Brands can derive value for an advertiser. With proper care, businesses and organizations can create equity for their merchandise or business with the creation of a good brand. Chapter 3 continues with a discussion of the idea of brand maintenance. We offer suggestions on how to maintain that brand you have built and why it is a good idea to engage in brand maintenance. A full discussion of why branding is important to your marketing communications goals; issues involved with the insertion of branding into your advertising and IMC campaigns are also examined in this chapter.

The issue of where to place one's branding in the overall IMC plan is covered, followed by coverage of issues related to becoming a brand leader. The issue of using branding to increase sales and market share are explained, and at the end of the chapter we have provided a summary via bullet points. As the reader now has a good understanding of what branding is, it is time to focus on the development of the advertising plan. In chapter 4 we focus on just that.

Chapter 4's coverage and discussion involves the development of an advertising plan. Issues and knowledge that you will have gleaned from the first three chapters are now ready to put into play. In order to make sure the reader understands the concepts and subjects that the authors have put forth, the chapter opens with an overview and definition of integrated marketing communications and its integration with the advertising process.

Next, we have created a summary of the stages necessary for the development, completion, and execution of an advertising campaign. The advertising plan is covered based upon each of the stages used to create the plan. The early portion of the chapter provides information and tips that should be used when you create your plan. You will note that all the tools you will need have, by this point, been provided. The length of the plan and the sections that should be included are also given coverage. As the book progresses, each of the stages in the advertising plan are presented, along with a quick summary of each section or stage. Because a lot of information and data are needed for the development of the plan, chapter 4 has been expanded to ensure there is enough information for the reader to be able to access the information and place that information into the advertising plan. Brief coverage of the media plan, and where the media plan fits into the overall advertising plan, is also provided.

The chapter ends with a transition into the subject of media basics. One of the hardest things to learn about media is those pesky media terms. Media vocabulary is different than most other industry vocabulary. Media planners and buyers use a lot of acronyms, and they have shortened versions of many words and word combinations. The authors have attempted to demystify those terms in chapter 5.

Chapter 5 opens by taking a look at what the term "media" really means; a discussion of "what is media" can be found the first page. The following section of the chapter discusses the issue of creating a media mix by first defining what that term means. This coverage is followed by a discussion of the options available to the advertising planner when it comes to selecting or utilizing various media outlets.

Each of the available media are looked at and probed. The positives of each of these media, as well as the downsides of each, are also provided. Coverage is focused here on print media, broadcast media, outdoor media, and cybermedia. The chapter continues with in-depth coverage of the factors, variables, and issues that may have an impact on an entrepreneur's selection of which type or types of media to use. Each of these factors is discussed with a focus on their impact on the media mix.

Budgeting is a big concern for entrepreneurs. Oftentimes, budgeting is the least enjoyable part of an entrepreneur's job. In reality, budgeting is not that bad. In fact, we feel that it may become one of your favorite areas of business and advertising. Budgeting allows an advertiser to control the overall advertising campaign from a financial point of view, thus providing value to the advertiser and entrepreneur. From our point of view, an understanding of budgeting is essential for the effective exploitation of a targeted market. As such, we have provided a lot of coverage for budgeting. We will expose you to the concept of budgeting in the first few chapters, and then we reinforce that concept once again in chapter 5 in the section "How Much Should I Budget for Media Expenses?"

Chapter 5 ends with some hints on how to maximize the return on your advertising investment. In advertising we refer to this as the return on advertising investment (ROAI). If you do not know how well your media are performing, you really do not have a plan at all. The chapter is summarized and the reader is ready to move on to the next chapter to dig deeper into the subject of advertising media.

Chapter 6 is called "Choosing and Executing Your Media Plan." While in the earlier chapters we discussed where the media plan belongs, in this chapter we provide a discussion of how to create and execute a media plan. Keep in mind that timing is essential in advertising, and even more so as you begin to take a look at your media plan. In chapter 5, we provide basic media information. We begin the coverage by explaining the concept of a media mix. In chapter 6, we begin the chapter by taking that media mix and turning it into a media plan. The chapter discusses the size and shape of an advertising program and why they are important for the media plan. Issues and terminology used in the industry are provided as part of that section. Size issues for the various media are covered, as are the various shapes that can be used in the media (but usually restrict) are also examined.

This coverage is followed by a discussion of when and where these sizes and shapes are available in the various media. The question we get regularly is "How much of each medium should be utilized by advertisers?" Because there is a need to answer that question, chapter 6 provides some detailed information about how much is enough (or too much, for that matter). Metrics used to calculate just how much coverage is needed in each of the media are provided, and a discussion on gross rating points (GRPs) and the formula used to calculate them is included.

Campaign length is very important to advertisers, so the chapter also touches on the ideal length of an advertising campaign. Once again, we provide some coverage of the budget followed by a lot of discussion of when and how to place advertising. Contract information and coverage rounds out that section. The chapter continues with some lengthy information about the concept of "flighting." When an advertiser places their media plan down on paper, that plan is known as a "flight," or a flight plan. We have provided a sample of a flight plan in order for the reader to see and understand what such a plan looks like. Additionally, the reader can use our sample as a template and create to his or her own flight plan or media schedule.

Chapter 6 ends with an overview of the use of nontraditional media. These media can be effective if used in an integrated fashion with other IMC executions. As we finish our planning discussion for the advertising, IMC, and media plans, we begin to take a look at the development of our creative executions, the message you want to send. Chapter 7 covers the issues involved with the development of the correct message to send to the correct audience. We have called this chapter "Crafting Your Message."

Because message content is so important to an advertiser, we felt that ample coverage was needed to ensure that the reader knows how to craft their message. Issues involved with the message development are detailed in chapter 7. This chapter begins with a broad category section titled "Great Ideas are Plentiful." Even though we all have good ideas for advertising, we want to make sure that these ideas translate to sales. In this chapter, we provide guidance and advice in terms of providing information that will help you to increase your chances of creating an effective message. In fact, we show you how to develop your creative strategy. We follow this up with information on how to become creative and how to let your creative juices flow in a section we call "Now for the Good News . . ."

We have generated many great ideas in this chapter, in hopes that they will inspire you to develop your *creative brief*. The creative brief is an outline (simplified) of your campaign objectives, target market, key influencers, competitors, product/service offerings and features, your single basic benefit, your supporting benefits, tome of the advertising, current audience perception and behaviors, desired audience perception and behaviors, your desired action from your market, and, finally, what we call "necessary musts." Each of these elements is covered in depth in this section.

We continue the chapter with hints and information on how to create your *unique selling proposition* (or USP). We follow this coverage with some information on the important aspects of your ad(s). Finally, we discuss the elements of an ad and how they impact final advertising executions. Because this information may be somewhat new to you, we have provided some information about how to be creative and addressed how to use (and where to get) outside assistance. We also suggest that you utilize the chapter on outside suppliers for help. As we summarize the chapter, we segue into chapter 8, where we provide some material on how to integrate all of your other marketing communications components into your executions.

As stated before, it is essential that an advertiser take a look at all of the possible tactics that can be used to reach out to and communicate with a target market and audience. As such, chapter 8 provides information on integrating other marketing communications components into your executions. The chapter begins by looking at the various marketing communications mix variables that are available, such as advertising, branding, cybermarketing, direct marketing, personal selling, public relations/publicity, and sales promotion(s). Since we have already covered the issues of branding and advertising in quite a bit of depth, we begin the discussions in this chapter with the concept of cybermarketing. Each of the areas of cybermarketing are discussed, and the positives and negatives associated with this execution approach are provided. Little-covered areas, such as electronic data interchange (EDI), are also given some attention.

Next, the chapter moves on to look at the issues involved in direct marketing. What is direct marketing, when should we use it, and why should it be used are major aspects of this section. With the rapid advances in communication and technology, database marketing is growing in importance. Here, we have developed and shared a section on what database marketing and how it can be used.

Personal selling and its impact on communication is also covered. The advantages of personal selling are highlighted and discussed. Since "public relations builds brands and advertising sustains brands," we thought it to be important that we offer some coverage of public relations and the use of publicity. Each of these areas is covered, as is the integration of these areas into integrated marketing communications plan for effective and more efficient advertising. Sales promotions and the types of sales promotions (i.e., trade versus consumer) are the topics of the final section.

Chapter 9 is one of the key chapters of the book. In chapters 1 through 8 we provided the keys for developing a basic advertising and IMC framework to help business owners create and execute research and market-based integrated marketing and advertising communications. In chapter 9, we offer the information necessary to create an overall IMC plan. Chapter 9 is titled "Putting the Plan Together and Measuring Its Effectiveness." If you do not know how well your plan is doing, you may as well not create a plan at all. In this chapter, we look at ways we can measure the effectiveness of an advertising and IMC campaign, not just by total sales, but by other metrics as well.

Chapter 8 begins with a summary of the first eight chapters. After the overview, we get right down into looking at the final step in advertising, which is the evaluation of the campaign. Information is given on the valuable output you can expect from your ability to measure your effectiveness. We then take a look at the issue of either doing it yourself or outsourcing the evaluation function. Hints are given on things one should evaluate as part of the campaign, not just the sales. We also provide you with some sources where you can obtain comparative data, should you decide to undertake the evaluation function yourself.

If you want to do it yourself, we show you an outline of the steps necessary for the undertaking of an evaluative research study. Step-by-step instructions are provided that will strengthen the quality and value of your research. At the end of the chapter, you will have all of the tools necessary to create an advertising, IMC, or media plan. Additionally, you will have the knowledge necessary to assess your campaign and plan and to correct the plan for more effectiveness. The chapter ends with an bulleted summary of the research and assessment process.

In the final chapter, we have provided information and discussion on the future of entrepreneurial advertising. The chapter opens with an overview of the current state of advertising, followed by one of the most important concepts for advertisers: environmental scanning. Environmental scanning is defined and discussed here, and the reasons that business owners must be involved in the undertaking of environmental scanning are also examined. A process for undertaking environmental scanning is then presented.

Potential changes in the advertising environment and landscape are the focus of the next section of the chapter, as we examine and discuss some of the changes occurring in our field. The issue of trying to stay current with this industry is looked at, as is the movement toward social media and the exploitation of those media by advertisers. A few final thoughts are offered and the chapter is summarized.

As both of us continue to work in the advertising field, and as we travel around giving presentations, have client meetings, get involved in our trade groups, teach students, and simply work at what we love, we find that we often hear the same questions asked about our industry. In an attempt to answer the most common questions we are asked, combined with those tougher questions, we have developed this book for entrepreneurs. We feel that the contents of the book will help any entrepreneur in his or her quest for personal and professional success. We are not claiming that this book alone will be responsible for that success, but rather that you, as a motivated reader and entrepreneur, will use the book as a guide in the development of your advertising and integrated marketing communications plan. By creating a partnership between the two of us and you, we are certain that your business, and in particular your advertising, will increase your business base, alleviate your time burdens, and make you the newest professional in the advertising and communications industry.

WHY YOU SHOULD READ THIS BOOK

Advertising for entrepreneurs is a difficult topic, in that everyone seems to think they are advertising experts. This book provides information and suggestions for your advertising to really deliver the audiences you want. Nothing happens in business until customers visit your business. This is true for both online and traditional brick-and-mortar businesses. The same holds true for entrepreneurs involved in service businesses. The product or service must be exposed to your potential audience. Read this book to see how to build your brand and create the best advertising possible. Find out when the time is right to look for outside suppliers.

All of the tools you need for the effective advertising for your products, services, and brand can be found in the following pages.

Enjoy the read!

What Is Advertising, and How Does It Fit into the Marketing Plan?

As you speak to colleagues, friends, and family, it may appear that everyone knows how to create effective advertising. This could not be further from the truth. The fact is that most people see the end product of an effective advertising campaign: the commercial. The development of that commercial message takes a lot of time and effort in order to make sure the message speaks to the audience, is created in a consistent manner, integrates with all other aspects of the marketing communication plan, is placed in the right advertising vehicles, and that it is placed at the correct time. In the end, the response to that message should be measured, if possible, or at least evaluated after the placement of the ad to see if, how, and to what degree the advertisement worked.

In order to create an outstanding advertising campaign, entrepreneurs must develop a research-based integrated marketing communication (IMC) plan that provides synergy and integration for the entrepreneur and generates the most bang for the buck. This chapter concentrates on how advertising fits into a business and marketing plan, and provides an overview of the entire book.

INTRODUCTION

Advertising is a complex and time-consuming process that must be undertaken if you want to succeed in business. Just developing a wonder product, in and of itself, will not make you successful. You must communicate the fact that you have the product available for consumers and you must establish a reason why the consumer should purchase the product or service.

This chapter looks at advertising's place in the business and marketing plan, and provides an overview of the advertising planning process. Let's begin with a working definition of advertising.

ADVERTISING DEFINED

When you hear the word "advertising," many different thoughts are likely to go through your mind. People define advertising in different ways, often along with the term "marketing." Advertising is *not* marketing; rather, advertising is a tactic that is used by marketers to communicate messages to their customers and other stakeholders. For the purposes of this book, we will define advertising in the following way:

A. The job of advertising is to provide the best possible selling message to the right target audience at the best possible price.
B. Advertising is paid. Because advertisers pay for advertising, they have full control of the content and media placement of the ad.
C. Advertising is an impersonal communication process. In other words, advertising is placed in various media to reach the correct audiences. With advertising, media are used to reach large numbers of people with one campaign.

Advertising can take two forms: institutional advertising and product advertising. *Product advertising* focuses on making consumers aware of an idea, product, or service and how that product may satisfy the consumers' needs or wants. *Institutional advertising* is used to make consumers aware of an organization or business and does not focus on a specific product, idea or service, but rather focuses on the business or organization itself.

The basic purpose of advertising is to inform, persuade, and/or remind customers of business and organizational offerings, such as products or services. Advertising can create an immediate response (e.g., "only two days left in the sale") or can be used to keep the product and/or business/organization's name in front of the consumer so that consumers remember the product, service, or organization when they are out shopping. Advertising should attempt to develop product or company loyalty, provide information to ease the customer's decision-making process, and develop awareness among the targeted group about potential offerings that are available to consumers. As an entrepreneur, you want to make sure that customers are aware of your business offerings and that they see your products and/or services as the best option when they decide to purchase.

When developing your advertising plan, be sure you keep the following in mind:

A. Tell people that you exist.
B. Let your audience know what products and services are available to them.
C. Let your customers know where you are located, and provide directions if you are located in an obscure location.
D. Tell your audience the reason why they should purchase from you, as opposed to opting for other products. We will discuss this concept in more detail chapter 7. This process is known as the development of your *Unique Selling Proposition* (USP).

ADVERTISING'S ROLE WITHIN THE MARKETING PLAN

Although advertising has been around for a long time (since 1655, by many accounts), it has metamorphosed into a combination of science and art. The current state of the art places the execution of advertising into the IMC mix.

IMC attempts to use various tactics to communicate with internal and external customers in a way that creates synergy among all IMC variables and provides additional impact and value to the advertiser. As such, advertising is often partnered with other types of marketing communication (MARCOM) such as personal selling, sales promotion, cybermarketing, direct marketing, public relations and publicity, and branding.

Because advertising is a type of marketing execution or tactical execution, it is one of the *last* tasks that are undertaken by businesses. The marketing communications plan (which includes the advertising) should be a logical extension of the company's marketing plan, and it should provide executions that are in line with the company's objectives, mission, vision, and strategy. When you take a look at a marketing plan, it should provide direction for the development and execution of the advertising and IMC programs.

THE MARKETING PLAN

Often, it is easier to understand this concept within the context of the marketing planning process. The following steps are generally used in marketing planning, and should be reviewed prior to undertaking the advertising and IMC planning processes. The following outline provides an overview of marketing planning and indicates where the advertising/IMC functions are undertaken.

THE MARKETING MANAGEMENT PROCESS

The company mission statement
The company vision statement
Company/Organizational/Corporate objectives
Situation analysis/Marketing opportunity analysis
Target market
Marketing objectives
Marketing strategy:

    Restate the target market
    Analysis of buyer behavior in the market
    Market segmentation analysis

Marketing tactical executions

    Product development and management
    Price development and management
    Channels of distribution (including supply chain management and logistics)
    Integrated marketing communications (IMC), oftentimes called "MARCOM" (marketing communications).

(Continued)

> The total marketing program, including resource allocations and
> budgets.
> Evaluation, control and response of the target market to the marketing
> initiatives.

If we use a summary approach when looking at each of these task areas, a better understanding of the process of creating great IMC and IMC's integration with all of the other elements of marketing becomes clearer.

It is essential for entrepreneurs and their employees to know why the company is in business. The development of a company mission statement helps with this process. Mission statements should be grounded in the present and offer employees, managers, owners, and customers a glimpse of what the company does.

Equally important is a company's vision statement. The vision of a company provides direction for future product/service developments and direction for the company's advertising and IMC management. A vision statement looks to the future and reports how a company would like to see itself and how it would like its customers (both internal and external) to see it.

Company, organizational, and corporate objectives are important. IMC and marketing are driven by the objectives set out by the company. In advertising, it is essential to know exactly why the advertising material is being developed. Many companies have immediate, medium, and long-term objectives; an IMC plan helps to make sure that these objectives are achieved. Business owners should ensure that the objectives are measurable and time-restricted, as these will later be used to measure the effectiveness of the marketing and IMC programs.

A situational analysis provides an in-depth history of a company or organization. It provides data on company products, sales, profits, and a history of the company's development. It should include successful and nonsuccessful endeavors, to allow IMC developers to understand what has worked, and what has not, in the past. One important part of the situational analysis is environmental scanning. Because the only constant in the universe is change, entrepreneurs must be on top of any changes that are occurring in the environments in which they do business. There are many different types of programs that undertake environmental scanning, so entrepreneurs must develop the system that works best for them. From the environmental scanning program, strategic responses can be identified and developed to best solve problems associated with changes in the environment(s).

A marketing opportunity analysis should be undertaken to narrow the choices an entrepreneur has in regard to which markets to enter. Because of the limitations of time, money, and human resources, it is best to target one (or a few) groups of customers in order to take advantage of the lower costs associated with the targeting process. As such, marketers need to have information on the various markets available to enter.

A target market includes all customers who may have a need or desire for your product, are willing to buy your product, and have the ability to make a purchase (oftentimes this relates to having the financial wherewithal to purchase, but this may not always be the case).

Specific objectives, which are measurable, time-bound, and are specific to marketing, need to be developed. Think about why you are in business and what you hope to accomplish by developing your marketing and IMC plan(s).

Taking into consideration the big picture of what you hope to accomplish with your marketing and the total directional thrust of your marketing program is called the *marketing strategy*. Within the strategy, restate your target market, research how your market behaves, and then assess the need for market segmentation. Segmentation may be necessary because the target market is too large for an entrepreneur with limited resources. It is a good idea to explore segmenting your market if this is the case. Different buyers have different wants and needs, and they likely have different methods of purchasing products. It is beneficial for any entrepreneur to have a thorough understanding of his market. For example, if it is found that all customers purchase the same way, he may want to utilize a mass marketing approach. This approach is often used in business-to-business (B2B) marketing. If the customers react differently to the marketing approaches (i.e., they have different methods of buying, have different wants and needs, or different product uses), then it might make sense to divide the target market into segments and create different marketing programs for each. This approach also allows business owners to see who the heavy, medium, and light users of a product or service are, and to allocate marketing resources according to the impact of each of these market segments.

The tactical executions are where the rubber hits the road. Programs must be developed for each of the controllable variables available to an entrepreneur. Controllable variables allow an entrepreneur to reach and serve target market(s) and to do battle with competitors. The four controllable variables and tactical executions to keep in mind are: product development and management, the development of effective and integrated channels of distribution, the development of prices that are palatable to the customers, yet generate profits and sales for the entrepreneur, and the development of a comprehensive IMC plan.

All of the micro-plans developed above should be placed into *one* marketing program. The marketing program, in turn, should provide integration and synergy between each of the steps involved in marketing planning. Additionally, budgets should be developed and resources (both capital and human) allocated to each of the tasks required to complete and execute the marketing plan.

It is essential that an entrepreneur have a mechanism to make sure all marketing is working. The easiest way to accomplish this is through a program that watches the response of the target market. Look back at your objectives. Were each of the objectives achieved? Which ones were not? Why not? Did you exceed your objectives? Why or why not? Once you have answers to these questions, readjust your marketing dollars as needed and continue with your program.

As outlined above, advertising is a small, but essential, part of the overall marketing plan. Additionally, advertising falls into the IMC plan and must integrate and work seamlessly with the other IMC variables. Chapter 4 will examine where advertising fits into the IMC mix and how it can be integrated with other elements to create effective and cost-efficient communications that will drive customers to your business.

A MARKETING PLAN TEMPLATE

Now it is time for you to develop your marketing plan. If you already have one completed, run an audit to make sure that you have all crucial elements in place for the plan. If you do not yet have a completed marketing plan, just fill in the blanks below. Keep in mind that the more complete and comprehensive your marketing plan is, the less work you will have when it comes to developing your IMC and advertising plans. There is one last but important point to remember: keep you work as brief as possible. Including charts and graphs (or figures and tables) will help show you your marketing map without having to include a lot of verbiage. A picture can tell a thousand words!

THE MARKETING PLAN TEMPLATE

Be sure to fill in the blanks completely based upon your current marketing plan. If you have never completed a marketing plan, fill in the blanks with as much information as you have. You should always be adding new information to the plan, and will have ample time ahead to continue to add information and data to your plan.

Why are you in business? Mission statement:
Where do you see yourself in the next 5, 10, or 20 years? Vision Statement:
What does your business hope to achieve over the next year? Five years? Ten years? Corporate/Organizational Objectives:
Now, provide a comprehensive snapshot of the history of your company/organization. Be sure to include how you will assess changes in the environment, and how you will respond to them (environmental scanning). Situational analysis:
Which markets appear to offer you the best opportunity to turn a profit and remain successful? Market opportunity analysis (MOA):
Who are your customers? What do they look like as people (we often include an actual photo or illustration of a typical person from the

(Continued)

target market or audience)? What features do your typical customers have? What do they look like as people? Target market:

What do you hope to achieve by instituting a marketing program? Make sure these are time-bound, specific to marketing, and measurable/quantifiable. Marketing objectives:

What overall strategy (or strategies) do you want to employ to provide direction for your marketing activities? Marketing strategy:

What lines of attack are you developing for your marketing mix? Tactical executions: Product planning/Development/Management pricing

Which distribution channels will most effectively reach your targeted market? Will you be using a logistics plan? Supply chain management? Channels of distribution development:

Which of the communication variables will you employ? IMC mix:

Cybermarketing (or online marketing)
Personal selling
Direct marketing
Branding
Advertising
Public relations/Publicity
Sales promotion

RECAP

In chapter 1 we introduced you to the subject of advertising. Additionally, we spent time recapping the concept of marketing and where advertising and the IMC mix fit into the overall marketing planning process. Each of the elements of the marketing plan was covered and discussed, and a template for the development of a marketing plan was presented at the end of the chapter. Hopefully, you have gotten a good start on your marketing plan and are ready to move on toward the development of your advertising plan and the execution of your marketing plan. The advertising plan will come to fruition in chapter 9.

With your marketing plan in hand, you now need to develop your advertising and IMC plan(s). Prior to discussing the advertising and IMC planning documents, chapter 2 will give you an overview of sources of information to help with your plans' development. Additionally, chapter 2 includes information about the decision of whether or not to outsource some of your marketing and advertising (IMC) activities. Oftentimes, it is wise for an entrepreneur to outsource some of her marketing efforts to independent contractors. Indeed, outsourcing may actually save time and effort, as well as cash, when it comes to creating and executing effective plans that deliver! Chapter 3 discusses the importance of branding in the marketing communications function and explains where branding will fit into the overall IMC process. In chapter 4, you will actually create an advertising plan. Keep reading, and good luck!

This chapter has shown you all of the steps necessary to generate an effective IMC and advertising plan. Specifically, we looked at:

- A definition of advertising
- Marketing's role within a firm
- Advertising's role within marketing
- A complete explanation of and template for the advertising process.

Information for each of the steps can be found throughout the book, so if you need help with any of the sections, read ahead (or back, depending on your needs).

The remainder of the book will provide information on how to create the most effective advertising to drive sales and make your business a success.

SUMMARY

☑ In advertising, you must communicate the fact that you have the product(s) or service(s) available for consumers, and you must establish a reason why the consumer should purchase the product or service from you.

☑ Remember that advertising is a paid, impersonal communications process.

☑ Advertising can be used to influence the consumer's decision-making process.

☑ Your advertising plan is part of your overall marketing plan; similarly, advertising is just one element of your entire IMC effort.

2

Outside Suppliers
and Other Sources of Help

As advertising and marketing consultants and professionals, we are often asked about outsourcing projects for businesses and organizations. Additionally, we are constantly asked for advice on how to start a business. We can offer one great piece of advice for those who are entrepreneurial in spirit . . . outsource when necessary! We suggest that anyone who starts a business make sure that they have the three necessary competencies in place: (1) Marketing, (2) Finance, and (3) Legal expertise. It is essential to begin your new venture by making sure you have all three of these basic business essentials.

Many people feel that they can be everything to their business. We are here to tell you that "it ain't so." You know your competencies and, although you may have more knowledge than the average bear, you do not have the time to utilize everything you know. The answer is to outsource many of your tasks and duties. Outsourcing allows you to generate additional expert advice for your business while the same time, if done correctly, it will help you to save money.

This chapter probes the issues of when and who to hire as outside suppliers of data, information, products, and advice. We will offer additional sources of help for the do-it-yourselfer, although we still feel that many of your functions should be outsourced.

OUTSIDE SUPPLIERS

As previously stated, there are many times when it may be to your advantage to access outside suppliers of products and services. In particular, due to the complex nature of advertising, we recommend that you make overtures toward local, regional, or national advertising agencies. Many agencies specialize in your type of business. The key is to understand when, why, and where you should utilize additional expertise.

Typically, small entrepreneurs serve as their own advertising departments. If you are a small or medium sized enterprise (SME), you may have a somewhat larger advertising department; however, it will likely only have two or three people working to cover this very difficult area. In order to ensure that you are spending your hard earned dollars effectively, you must understand advertising and marketing. Additionally, you must have the time to spend on this function. Thus, if you are short on time and/or need more expertise, you may want to consider outsourcing a significant portion (if not all) of your advertising. We recommend that you continue to have someone on your payroll who will oversee the function of advertising and marketing communication, however, in order to save time and money associated with these functions, we recommended that you outsource and hire an advertising or marketing communication agency.

Outside suppliers are unique in that they offer an outside view. Business owners often become advertising myopic when perform all functions themselves. There is a saying in advertising: "We have met the consumer and they ain't us." Bringing in new eyes, ideas, thoughts, education, and so on can make your advertising campaigns much more effective. The other side of outsourcing is that businesses often save money by generating better advertising than they have been doing in-house.

The first step in trying to decide if you need an outside supplier is to conduct an internal inventory of what you want your advertising to achieve. We recommend answering the following questions prior to hiring an agency:

1. What types of information are needed so that you may advertise more effectively?
2. What role do you want your in-house personnel to play in regard to your advertising?
3. What is the time frame, or urgency, in getting the advertising completed?
4. What is your time frame for undertaking advertising research, development, and design?
5. How do you currently exploit any economies of scale that deal with your advertising?
6. What is your advertising budget? Do you have budget constraints?
7. Do you have the available expertise to handle advertising yourself?
8. Do you have the manpower to accomplish all of your tasks in the time allowed?

It is essential that you understand the answers to the above questions. Also, make sure that you do not skip any of the questions, as doing so may cause you may end up with a less than efficient advertising plan. One of our smaller clients once called us to help him develop an advertising campaign. The client, Jorge, wanted to open a new, upscale restaurant in Albuquerque, New Mexico. Jorge wanted to create a state-of-the-art advertising campaign to would drive large numbers of new customers into his establishment. We provided Jorge with the above questions for him to answer. It is essential that you understand the environment in which you work if you want to get the biggest bang for your marketing buck.

Jorge called and indicated that he has satisfactorily answered all of the above questions. In fact, he had answered all of the questions but number six, the budget question. While we were meeting with him, Jorge told us of all the requirements he had for the advertising. Additionally, he told us in which media to place the advertisements, and he even told us when to advertise. Jorge asked us to prepare a "down and dirty" advertising campaign that would follow his plan. We did. Upon returning to Jorge's place of business, we showed him the work we had completed. Jorge was very excited about the amount of work we had put in, and he loved the media flighting plan (which we will explain to you in a later chapter). What he was not excited about were the costs associated with advertising. His plan called for complete coverage of his market area, however cost for the media placements alone exceeded his budget by over $75,000. Needless to say, Jorge went back to the drawing board to scale down his plans. The lesson or moral to this story: Make sure you answer all of the above questions to save yourself frustration, time, and money.

After answering these questions (and remember, we are all in different environments and have different needs and wants, so the answers to these questions should be unique to each person and company), it is time to look at some attributes you will want in an agency (or from other outside suppliers of information). There are many different types of suppliers of advertising services. Perhaps you only need media placement. Perhaps you are only interested in the development of your ad creative. It may be that you need a full-service agency. If you have a need for public relations (PR), advertising, technology help, sales promotions, personal selling, data, additional personnel, or the like, you should know that there are other companies and organizations that specialize in meeting these needs.

We suggest the following three considerations when choosing outside suppliers:

1. The supplier must have a system of communication. There must be a system built to maximize the effective integration of your marketing communications variables.
2. You must place a high level of importance, or status, on that supplier.
3. You want a supplier that offers independence. In other words the supplier should be free from internal threats from higher ups. As we mentioned earlier, it is great to have a new pair of eyes come in and assess your current advertising or integrated marketing communications (IMC) program.
4. Make sure to compose a list of all services needed.
5. Create a rating rubric to help you remember important information about the agency or supplier.
6. Check all published sources in regard to who and what is available in your area.
7. Make sure you are comfortable with the agency you choose.
8. Finally, determine if the agency will be able to handle all of your needs; otherwise, you may have to find additional agencies to provide you with additional services.

TYPES OF EXTERNAL SUPPLIERS OF ADVERTISING ASSISTANCE

The most obvious type of supplier is an advertising agency. Hiring an agency to provide advertising and IMC services may seem like a simple matter, but it may not be. Advertising and IMC agencies often specialize in different services. Not all agencies are full service. Listed below are the main types of advertising agencies.

1. *The full-service agency.* Full service agencies offer their clients all of the services necessary to carry out total IMC functions (i.e., planning, ad creation, ad production, media placement, and, often, an evaluation of the effectiveness of the campaign). Additionally, full-service agencies often offer marketing services such as marketing research, brand reviews, competitive analysis, sales promotion planning, creation and execution, and other services.

2. *Full-service specialty agencies.* Specialty agencies specialize in some type of business. For example, certain agencies are experts at B2B advertising, health care advertising, sports and/or entertainment, tourism, retailing, or industries.

3. *Media buying services.* Often, smaller firms (and also very large firms) specialize in nothing but buying and placing media for their clients.

4. *A la carte agencies.* A la carte agencies offer their clients, for a fee, any services they need. Typically the expertise is in media and/or creative services. These agencies may create a logo, tagline, weekly newspaper inserts, or other piece of marketing collateral.

5. *Independent creative boutiques.* These agencies specialize in the development and production of creative executions for their clients. Creative executions are the tactical executions of marketing that turn into print, TV, radio, and other advertisements.

6. *Outside, freelance consultants.* In any given area, advertising professionals are willing to help you for a fee. These people are employed typically by someone else and moonlight by helping their clients become successful. Professors of advertising and marketing (as well as other fields) typically are involved in business consulting and can be a great source of help.

In addition to advertising agencies, you may require a number of other service providers. For example, marketing research companies are available to help study markets and make recommendations in regard to your overall marketing and advertising planning. Getty Images is an international company that provides videos, photographs, and other types of creative assistance (for a fee). There are companies that offer sales people as an outsourced service. Local media outlets in many areas have professionals on staff to assist businesses with their advertising needs.

Other important and often overlooked sources of service are database management and marketing companies. Customer relationship management has become an increasingly effective tool for low-budget advertisers, and we recommend that you look into the option of using these specialists. Furthermore, there are agencies and companies that specialize in direct response advertising. They often can provide additional help in assisting you with developing your merchandising and point-of-sale displays.

Do not forget to look into utilizing any and all marketing research companies available to you. Good marketing and advertising research can create high sales and traffic for your business. Trade associations are helpful, and often provide reports and assistance to their members. Additionally, do not overlook your ability and opportunities to network with other people in your position and find out what they have done to help their advertising programs. Finally, academic consultants (such as professors or other education professionals) are often less expensive than other business people and can provide sound, cutting-edge advertising advice and help.

Depending on your needs, any or all of these suppliers may be of service to you and your business. The question that next should come to mind is, "When and why would I want to retain outside provider services?"

We have found that the following four concepts will help guide you in regard to when (and why) to use external suppliers.

A. You want to establish credibility for your product, service, or organization. As such, you may want to use external suppliers to give a third-party endorsement of your business. Consumers look to other people to help them make decisions. It is much stronger to say that you won a J. D. Power and Associates Award, which implicitly tells everyone how great your business is, than to tell all of your customers yourself how great you are. Of course your customers expect you to say nice things about your organization, but when J. D. Power says the same thing it carries much more weight.

B. You may not have the competence necessary to perform all of your advertising functions. If this is the case, you may want to find suppliers who have a particular expertise in an area you are exploring. If someone can do it better, for less money, and more effectively than you can, let them.

C. Contrary to popular belief, it is oftentimes much less expensive to outsource services than it is to have professionals on staff to perform those functions. If you can save money from outsourcing, do it!

D. Because the functions involved with advertising are so time-consumptive, it is often a good idea to maximize your efficiency by outsourcing. You may want some projects to be turned around faster than your in-house staff can provide, or perhaps you have an urgent project without available expertise. You also may not have the equipment necessary to create and execute many of the functions involved with advertising. Whatever the case, if you are looking for increased capacity, outsourcing may be your best answer.

SELECTING EXTERNAL SUPPLIERS

Once you have a good understanding of the advertising functions you would like to accomplish, you need to select those providers. In selecting your suppliers, we suggest following a few simple rules.

First, choose a supplier that will offer you some level of prestige. Many firms have high brand equity, and when stakeholders (customers, investors, bankers, etc.) see that you are using a high quality supplier, you add value to your brand!

Second, look for experience. What past experience does the provider have? Do they have particular expertise in a given area?

Third, look at the provider's personnel. Make sure the agency personnel have the right qualifications, skill base, and knowledge.

Finally, check on the costs associated with each of your tasks. What will the total cost be? What will be returned to you? We recommend that you develop or utilize a formula that gives you an indication of your return on your advertising investment.

We are confident that you will be able to select service providers that will generate additional sales and return a significant amount on your advertising investment.

There are many additional types of companies that provide advertising services. Typically, these companies and organizations deal with the data associated with the development and execution of an advertising campaign. The next section provides a cursory look at the top organizations involved in providing advertising data and information.

SUPPLIERS OF ADVERTISING AND MARKETING DATA AND INFORMATION

As stated above, there are many organizations that provide advertising and marketing data and information. Because the cost of these activities is prohibitive for many individual entrepreneurs, these companies compile and sell the applicable data to entrepreneurs, SMEs, Fortune 500 companies, advertising agencies, and others. Subscriptions to these data-offering organizations can run in the six figures depending on what type of information (and how much) you are looking for. The major providers of this information are listed and listed below, and a short description of the services they offer is also provided.

1. **Financial Information**
    a. *Funk and Scott Index of Corporations and Industries.* The Funk and Scott Index provides data and information on articles pertaining to finance and accounting. It is, essentially, a reader's guide to financial data and literature.
    b. *The Business Periodical Index.* The Business Periodical Index provides the same information as Funk and Scott, but focuses on *all* literature and articles in the business area.
    c. *Databases* (ProQuest, ABI/INFORM, etc.). Databases are useful for gaining access to lists of information. You can access a database much like you once used to access a library's card catalog. Type "ProQuest" into your Internet browser, and you will be taken to the ProQuest site. One word of caution, many of the databases require subscriptions. When you are ready to access any of the various databases, you will likely find that it is more cost-effective to use the databases that are found at your local college or public library.
    d. *The Wall Street Journal.* The *Journal* features current articles on business.

e. *Business Week.* Much like the *Wall Street Journal* in its coverage, *Business Week* is a trade magazine and provides up to date coverage of new happenings in business.

f. *Moody's manuals* (i.e., OTC, Industrial, Bank, and Financial). The Moody's corporation offers many different publications, or manuals, that provide volumes of financial and operating information for over 30,000 companies and 20,000 government entities. These are published annually, however updates are typically available weekly. Some of the publications include: *Moody's Industrial, Moody's Transportation, Moody's Public Utility, Moody's OTC (Over the Counter) Industrial, Moody's Bank and Financial, Moody's Municipal and Government, and Moody's OTC Unlisted.* The data are especially useful when you begin to develop your competitive analysis.

g. *Standard and Poor's.* Standard and Poor's provides financial data on 11,000 publicly traded companies. Typical manuals of publication include *Standard and Poor's Corporation Records, Over-the-Counter Regional Exchange Reports, American Stock Exchange Reports,* and *New York Stock Exchange Reports.* Standard and Poor's (or "S&P," as it is usually referred to) also publishes *The Daily News,* which provides up to date financial and stock information. Once again, these data are useful in the development of your competitive analysis.

h. *Hoovers (D&B).* Hoover's is a division of the D & B Corporation (formally Dun and Bradstreet), and gives a snapshot of thousands of businesses and organizations. It provides data on company leaders and company financials. It is also useful in developing your competitive analysis.

i. *Internal company publications* (i.e., annual reports, prospectuses, etc.). These provide information on the history of a company and company environments, both past and future. These sources of information and data are useful when establishing and maintaining your situational analysis.

j. *Donnelly Marketing Services.* Donnelly provides data and information in regard to various marketing issues with data pertaining to demo- and geographics. The information will help to build your overall advertising plan and supplement your situational analysis with useful data in regard to your competitors and physical market.

2. **Industry Information**

a. *Standard and Poor's Industry Surveys.* See above for a description.

b. *The U.S. Census* (http://www.census.gov). The U.S. government, by law, takes a survey of all of its residents every 10 years. Because of that, information about the United States market is plentiful. Each portion of the census focuses on specific areas of the United States. One can retrieve population data as well as business-specific data. Each of the publications holds a wealth of information and data that can be used in the development of an advertising campaign. Census data are free and are available online. The only caveat you must consider when using census data is that there are literally millions of pieces of data and information available; searching for specific data that are related to your business is a time-consuming task. Leave yourself a lot of time to search. It is best to log on to the census Web site and then explore as much as possible prior to actually trying to obtain the exact, specific information you are looking for! The various publications of the U.S. Census Bureau are provided below:

    i. The Census of Agriculture
    ii. The Census of Government
    iii. The Census of Business
    iv. The Census of Housing
    v. The Census of Construction Industries
    vi. The Census of Mineral Industries
    vii. The Census of Manufacturing
    viii. The Census of the Population
    ix. The Census of Transportation

  c. *The Thomas Register.* This source provides a lot of financial and personnel data about the various industries that are in operation. In addition it may help the marketer better understand their physical market by providing information and data in regard to the market as a whole (financial and other).

  d. *Donnelly Marketing Information Services.* As discussed above, Donnelly provides specific marketing information, however it has a cost associated with the acquisition of those data.

3. **The Four "-ics"** (geographics, demographics, psychographics, and behavioristics—all described in depth in chapter 4). The following sources will provide invaluable information for the development of your four "-ics."

  a. *The U.S. Census.* See above.

  b. *The Statistical Abstract of the United States.* Gives an overview of all statistics collected by the U.S. government. It will provide clues to you as to where to look for additional information.

  c. *State Statistical Abstracts.* Similar as the *U.S. Abstract,* only developed at the state level.

  d. *State governments.* State governments are often a good source for information regarding local markets. For example, an assessment of the taxes paid may help an entrepreneur to estimate her market size and market share.

  e. *Tax records.* These can be used as discussed above.

  f. *Licenses.* These will help to pinpoint who and where your customers are. For example, if you sell baby clothes, it may be a good idea to search the local birth records in order to determine who has been born, when, and where. You can add these pieces of information to your database and use them later for in customer relationship marketing executions.

  g. *County business publications.* Do not forget to access local and regional business publications. As residents of Allentown, PA, we really consult the *Eastern Pennsylvania Business Journal.* This publication provides a lot of up-to-date business information about our local market area. In addition, it publishes lists of regional businesses.

h. The *Sales and Marketing Management's Survey of Buying Power.* This is an excellent resource. *The Survey of Buying Power* is available to anyone who has a subscription to *Sales and Marketing Management* magazine. The survey shows the buying power of the United States as a whole, regions within the United States, counties, and cities within the counties. We highly recommend accessing this publication for a quick snapshot view of what business and economic activities are occurring in your area. For example, if you re involved in the sales of cars and trucks, the *Survey of Buying Power* will provide you with the amount and type of car and truck consumption in your market area, along with some sales information. The *Survey* provides advertisers with the buying power of a local area (or region), which can be used to help identify target audiences.

i. *Standard Rate and Data Services' (SRDS)* Lifestyle Market Analyst. This SRDS publication provides valuable psychographic information (lifestyle analysis). It helps advertisers to target their advertisements based upon a consumer's lifestyle.

j. *The Marketer's Guide to Media.* This is a useful publication that gives an abridged picture of what media are available in an area and at what costs. Remember, media pricing is are typically negotiated, so the *Marketer's Guide* simply allows readers to see the standard, list prices, for publications. It also helps marketers by providing a snapshot of ratings, listenership, and readership for the media (at both the national and local levels).

k. *Claritas.* This company uses a system it has named PRIZM (Potential Rating Index by Zip Markets) to help advertisers learn about the lifestyles that make up their customer base. Claritas has broken down over 500,000 neighborhoods into 40 basic clusters. Each of these clusters has been given a descriptive name. Advertiser can assess their customers' lifestyles by accessing PRIZM.

l. *Simmons Market Research Bureau (SMRB).* Simmons provides advertisers with detailed psychographic and business information that pertains to a business's markets. This is a useful source for helping to develop a customer analysis.

m. *Small business development centers.* Small Business Development Centers, or SBDCs, were developed by the U.S. Small Business Administration and offer help to small, local entrepreneurs. Most of the centers are headquartered at colleges and universities. These groups provide personal consulting, workshops, and programs. Many have newsletters. The centers can be accessed free of charge, but there may be a small fee for consulting assistance.

n. *Chambers of Commerce.* Chambers of Commerce are useful organizations that can provide local market data for the development of an advertising plan.

o. *Better Business Bureau.* Better Business Bureaus (or BBBs), help entrepreneurs search for and find reputable suppliers. They may also be able to provide data and information that will be useful in the development of your advertising plan.

p. *IRI (Information Resources, Inc.).* IRI provides scanner data for major consumer goods products. If you sell any national consumer products, it would be a good idea to access the IRI data to see where and how well your brands are performing in your market area.

4. **Media Data**

a. *SRDS.* As briefly discussed above, the Standard Rate and Data Service (or SRDS), provides standard rates and other important data (such as contact information and ratings) for all media. SRDS has organized their data based upon who it appeals to. Thus, if you are involved in the sale of consumer products, you may want to access the SRDS Consumer Publications Volume and Database. The following publications are available from SRDS. There is a charge to access SRDS online, or you may subscribe to their hard copy publications, which are listed below.

   1. Consumer Publications
   2. Business Publications
   3. Canadian Advertising
   4. Network Rates and Data
   5. Newspaper Rates and Data
   6. Print World
   7. Newspaper Circulations
   8. Sport Radio Rates and Data
   9. Spot Television Rates and Data
   10. Print Media

b. *The Editor and Publisher Market Guide*
c. A.C. Nielsen
d. Nielsen Media
e. Simmons Market Research Bureau (SMRB)
f. Small business development centers
g. Local media
h. *Brand Week* magazine
i. *Ad Week* magazine
j. *Advertising Age* (especially data on the leading national advertisers, which is called "LNA," for leading national advertisers)
k. The Standard Directory of Advertisers
l. The Standard Directory of Advertising Agencies
m. *Ad Week* publications
n. IRI

5. **Cybermarketing and Interactive Services**

a. Google
b. Yahoo!
c. Microsoft

6. **Trade Associations**

a. The American Association of Advertising Agencies (AAAA)
b. Point of Purchase Advertising International (POPAI)
c. Outdoor Advertising Association
d. American Marketing Association

e. Academy of Marketing Science
f. American Advertising Federation (it is useful to become a member of a local chapter)
g. Sales and marketing executives
h. SCORE (Although not a trade association, SCORE is an organization of retired business professionals that can assist you in your business development process and provide sources of information)

THE BEST CAMPAIGNS ARE RESEARCH-BASED

The development of an effective advertising campaign is research-based. As such, the data needed to create an effective campaign are numerous. This chapter looked at sources of information and suppliers of the same. The data that you will need to assemble will come in handy as you complete your plan. The data and information presented in this chapter should be used to fill in the blanks of your IMC and advertising plan, as they are presented in the following chapters.

Keep in mind, the more data you generate prior to executing the plan, the higher the quality of the plan. Additionally, by assembling data early in the planning process, a smart entrepreneur can convert those data into useful information that will also strengthen the overall plan. Finally, by taking care of this time-consuming task up front, entrepreneurs will leave time to tend to the day-to-day activities of running a business.

Specifically, this chapter examined:

- Outside suppliers
- Types of external suppliers
- Issues and tips related to the selection of external suppliers
- Lists of suppliers

We look forward to offering additional hints on the development of effective advertising during the coming chapters of this book.

SUMMARY

☑ While it is always tempting to keep functions of your business in your own hands, and you may feel reluctant to relinquish any duties to an outsider, remember that these outside sources are experienced professionals.
☑ Invest the time early on in finding the right professionals with whom you feel comfortable outsourcing your marketing and advertising functions.
☑ Finding the right advertising agency can be an invaluable experience saving you time and energy down the road.
☑ Any agency working with you needs and wants the advertising they produce to be as effective as you do. Your success is their success.
☑ Remember that working with outside suppliers is a business relationship. Keep it professional.

3

Brand Development

A brand is more than a name or a logo. It is far more than the box you put your product in, or the color of your building.

While most brands we recognize today are represented by a trademarked icon or logo, it is important to realize what went into creating that brand in order to understand why the brand has such value, or *equity*. For consumers, the value of your brand can be determined by the strength of your promise . . . a promise of a particular experience. You must then deliver on that promise through product attributes such as quality, cost, and availability.

WHAT IS A BRAND?

A brand, in its most profound sense, is a way of thinking—a belief system or a philosophy. When properly delivered to your existing and potential customers, a brand will transform a simple product or service into a staple need of a particular lifestyle, or even a necessity for those who share similar beliefs.

As an entrepreneur who wants to offer a new product or service, you may say to yourself, "I just want people to buy what I have to offer. I'm not worried about 'belief systems' or 'philosophies.'" But remember, as a new business you must ask yourself, "Why would anyone choose my product over another?" and "What differentiates me from my competitors?" With every increase in competition comes an increased demand to differentiate your product, and when your product is similar to your competitors' goods or services, your brand will be under even greater pressure.

The most effective brands are those that have developed out of the belief system of the creator, and/or the employee base. When everyone in your company or organization feels the same way about your product, and believes in delivering the same message to the public, your chances for success are the greatest.

It is important, when hiring, to take this into consideration. Isn't it always easier to work in an environment where everyone shares the same values and feels motivated to achieve the same results? To some degree, such an environment will create a higher comfort level, and, in an ideal situation, will also help everyone to get along. While holding common beliefs may not be a prerequisite when applying for a job, as a potential employee, applicants need to understand what motivates you, the employer; and what belief systems are in place in the company.

BRAND MAINTENANCE

A brand is not built and then left alone. A brand needs to be nurtured. Keep in mind that every day, whether it be you or your employees (or your marketing department or your accounting department), you are continuing to shape your brand, while at all times keeping a watchful eye on your consumer.

Unfortunately, your target market's needs can change as well. Those things that are important to your customer now may not be the things that are important to them 10 years from now. When built properly, your brand should force you to reexamine it regularly. Don't feel like you are going through this process because there is something wrong with your brand—this is a *completely healthy process*. It is so healthy, in fact, that if you involve your coworkers in the process, or a portion of them (such as all managers), you will, in the process, help to motivate them and show that they are an important part of the brand itself. You may also open the table for discussions that you normally would not have had. The following are examples of some questions to consider when undergoing a brand self-evaluation:

- What is your *brand essence*, or the promise of your brand, when summed up in its simplest terms? If you were Harley-Davidson, your brand essence would be *freedom* and *independence*. If you were Volvo, it would most likely be *safety*.
- Do consumers view your brand essence the same way you do? In other words, are consumers in agreement with what you say your brand stands for?
- How is your *brand awareness* within your target audience? Is recognition and recall of your brand at an acceptable and effective level?
- How much *brand equity* have you built?
- Is your brand legally protected? Is it trademarked?

There will be times beyond your control when you are forced to take a fresh look at your brand. Perhaps the consumer's mindset has changed drastically, the market you once dominated has moved on to other alternatives, or a competitor has released information that affects consumers' perception of your product.

Overcoming a negative impression associated with your brand can be a difficult task. Typically, it takes months, or even years, to build a single attribute into your brand, a perception that you have worked very hard to create. In the blink of an eye, however, that one positive attribute can quickly turn into a negative one . . . often beyond your control. This is when your brand needs you most, when you must engage in damage control.

Imagine, for example, a company that manufactures baby and toddler toys. That company has spent years building the perception that they are trustworthy and that their products are safe. The company has proved this through trials, research, and testimonials that they are at the top of their game and care strongly about their end user. They have become a leader in the industry, backed by moms, daycares, and health officials (oh . . . and of course kids) across the country. Then, one day, an isolated injury occurs, one that barely involves one of their products. The press misconstrues the story, and soon the company is faced with lawsuits, recalls, and, worst of all, a lack of trust from consumers. Imagine the impact of such an incident on your business *and your brand.* What kind of investment of time and money would it take to restore your brand to the way it was?

WHY IS BRANDING IMPORTANT TO MY MARKETING COMMUNICATIONS GOALS?

To best understand branding's role in your advertising, let's start by looking at it the other way around. it is your advertising that can have the most immediate influence on the public's *brand awareness* and your consumers' *brand loyalty.* It is also through your advertising that a more immediate change can be implemented to affect the perception of your brand, quicker with respect to other brand-influencing factors such as your sales force, public relations, packaging, or even the product itself. Every ad you run will leave the reader, viewer, or listener with some impression of your brand and your business. Likewise, every ad you run should be looked upon as an opportunity to continue to shape the perception of your brand in order to improve your brand equity.

As an entrepreneur, it is important to remember that brands matter, even when the advertising does not take a strong branding approach. For instance, you may be running a simple print ad with a special discount coupon for a particular item. What you cannot lose sight of is the fact that someone reading this ad will still see a logo, will feel a certain way about the ad, may even see or feel a certain personality coming from the ad, and, most importantly, will make some judgment on the quality of the ad, the offer, and your company.

WHERE DOES BRANDING FIT INTO MY IMC PLAN?

Branding, like advertising, is one element of an integrated marketing communications plan, as mentioned in chapter 1. However, your branding should be viewed as an ever-present sounding board for all of your marketing efforts. Branding thrives on consistency., and it is through brand management that you will set yourself up with guidelines (best put in the form of a written manual) to ensure consistency throughout all other IMC elements, from print advertising to personal selling, from public relations to direct marketing.

These guidelines can take on different forms. When formally put into place, branding guidelines should be a document describing tangible parameters such as color palettes, logo specifications, font requirements and treatments, tagline usage, and so on. Intangible brand attributes should also be noted as written reminders in these guidelines. Ask yourself, "How do I want my brand to be known?" Then, note these descriptors in your branding guidelines so that others can reference them. It may be as simple as adjectives like "convenient," "high-end," "safe," or "long lasting." It could also be words you want associated with your brand, such as "independence," "community," or "tradition." It is these buzzwords that will be the underlying message carried throughout your IMC plan.

BECOMING A BRAND LEADER

When executed properly, your IMC program should increase your market share and move your brand towards the front position within your industry. Depending on the amount of competition and the buying climate of your target market, this may be easier for some entrepreneurs than others. Success could depend greatly on the uniqueness of your product or service; it can also depend on how quickly trial purchases turn into repeat purchases, thus turning brand awareness into brand loyalty. Your goal is to be not only *top of mind* for all existing and potential customers, but also the product or service of choice within your industry or category. When this happens, you will have become a brand leader, and will be faced with the daunting task of maintaining that position.

EMOTIONAL CONNECTION

If you think that branding does not play a serious role in how consumers make an emotional connection with a company and its products, you are mistaken. Take, for example, the historic error in judgment made by one of the largest companies in the world, Coca-Cola. In 1985, when Coca-Cola introduced its New Coke, the reception was expected to be overwhelmingly positive. Two hundred thousand blind taste tests and $4 million in research leading up to the change had proven that New Coke would outperform both Pepsi and the existing Coke formulation. What Coke never could have foreseen was the outcry from the public and the resistance to change and the new product. It turns out that Coke had neglected the emotional value of their current brand to the American people. Coke never asked consumers how they would *feel* about the change when considering a change in the product, and thus betrayed the trust that they had worked so hard to build.

The value of a brand is just as important from an internal perspective as it is from the public perspective. Be sure to involve your employees and coworkers in new branding and advertising efforts right from the start. You can do this through a memo, or by circulating a notice. It can be posted in a lunchroom, or sent in a company-wide e-mail. Avis, with the help of its advertising agency at the time, used to put printouts of upcoming ads into employees' pay envelopes, thereby letting everyone see the campaign before it went public.

Internal communications displaying and explaining your branding and advertising efforts can add a great deal of value to the company when done on a large scale a. One idea for accomplishing this would be to gather your employees together for a meeting to make the announcement that the company is about to launch a new advertising effort. Show examples of the ads and allow your employees to engage the advertising and ask questions. This will help everyone to understand what is about to be seen by potential customers, and gets their buy-in on the campaign. This meeting could take on the form of a pep rally, in which you not only show off the new campaign, but also get people excited about the new effort. Everyone will be made to feel like they are part of the team, even if they had nothing to do with the development of the advertising. This is a great way to motivate employees, while at the same time helping to ensure that they are on board with the efforts and that they do not feel left out.

BRANDING ON A SHOESTRING BUDGET

As a start-up entrepreneurial business, you need to begin getting your name out into your community as quickly as possible. Along with building awareness, there is a need to begin shaping your brand as well. This will happen with every conversation you have, every form of communication you send, and every person who comes in contact with some part of your business. Keep an eye on everywhere that your company name, logo, or employees will have some presence or representation. Here are some tips for ways to begin building your brand:

- Join your local Chamber of Commerce. Most Chambers have a minimal annual membership fee, but the connections they offer to other business-people and community leaders can be invaluable. Attend mixers and work to expose Chamber members to your products or services. If applicable, host a mixer at your business.
- Always include your company's tagline and a key differentiating point (or single basic benefit) on your business card and in your e-mail signature.
- Write an article about your business or relevant to your industry and post it online through relevant e-zines, Web sites, and blogs.
- Create your own blog on a high-traffic site, such as Xanga or HubPages.
- Create a company page on social networking sites, such as Facebook or MySpace.
- Invite local media representatives to your business for a tour or interview. Include the business editor for any local newspapers and business journals, if your area has one.
- Be sure you are listed in any local directories relevant to your business, such as new resident publications and Welcome Wagon directories.
- Provide business cards, brochures, and discount offers to Realtors who can, in turn, pass them along to new area residents.

RECAP

In chapter 3, we addressed issues related to the concept of branding and focused on concerns that are important to the overall development and execution of a brand. We looked at the concepts associated with the development of a quality brand that has inherent brand equity built in. Additionally, we made an argument for the addition of branding as an element of the marketing communications mix by virtue of the brand's ability to operate as a silent salesperson at the point of sale.

Specifically, we examined:

- The definition and discussion of what makes a brand a brand
- Issues involved in the maintenance of a brand
- Why brand essence has value and the concepts associated with brand essence
- The creation of brand awareness
- Brand equity and its importance
- Why branding is so important in the development of an IMC plan
- Brand loyalty and its importance
- Methods involved in the development of making your brand a brand leader.

In chapter 4, we will insert the concepts of branding into the development of your advertising plan. Issues involved in planning and execution will be covered, and the process of integration will also be discussed.

SUMMARY

☑ A brand must be developed, maintained, and nurtured if you expect it to grow and succeed.

☑ Branding, like advertising, is just one element of the Integrated Marketing Communications effort and cannot take place in a vacuum.

☑ Successful branding does not require a large, dedicated budget; it can be accomplished effectively on a small budget. Dedication is more important than dollars.

☑ A key aspect of branding is to involve everyone in the company in the effort, making them aware of any advertising before it happens. The effects can be both positive and motivating.

4

Developing Your Advertising Plan

In chapters 1 through 3 we laid the groundwork for the development of your advertising campaign. In chapter 4, we will discuss one of the processes used for the development of an effective advertising campaign that delivers all of your objectives. The success of your plan depends on you. In chapter 1, we provided the basic concepts involved in advertising and marketing. Prior to embarking on your plan development, re-visit your marketing plan to make sure all of the elements are in place. The concepts we spoke about in chapter 1 will be used as the cornerstone of the advertising plan.

Chapter 2 provided you with sources of information in regard to your plans development. In chapter 3, we focused on the brand and why brand development will be so important during the next decade. An advertising plan should focus on the creation of a branding campaign and provide an outlet for speaking with your consumers and other stakeholders about your product and service offerings.

WHAT IS INTEGRATED MARKETING COMMUNICATIONS AND HOW DOES ADVERTISING FIT INTO THIS WHOLE PROCESS?

Prior to opening a discussion about the creation and development of a comprehensive advertising plan, we want to show you where advertising fits into the Integrated Marketing Communications (IMC) mix. As with marketing, IMC is also planned and executed. IMC planning provides entrepreneurs with direction and helps to keep them on task for the execution of all marketing communications tactics. Advertising is part of the IMC mix, and is the generally the most important element of the plan. Any time you, as an advertiser, want to speak to your *publics* (both internal and external), a message must be crafted and placed where the recipients can be exposed to it. The process of communications in business is referred to as IMC. Although IMC is a somewhat new concept, it makes sense (and dollars)! We will cover all aspects of IMC in chapter 8, but exposure to the concept earlier provides a basis for the advertising plan. Let's take a look at the IMC planning process before we begin working to develop your advertising plan.

IMC Defined

The basic concept of IMC, whether it is called marketing communication management (MARCOM) or integrated marketing communications (IMC) is to talk to audiences using a clear and consistent message. Doing this provides additional continuity and value for the communications activities that you will develop for your business. Additionally, by measuring IMC, you can get a better picture of the return from your advertising and IMC investments (also known as ROAI, Return on Advertising Investments).

Although advertising is the main communications tactic for entrepreneurs, there is great value in developing a full IMC plan. Because the concept of IMC will be covered in a future chapter, we would simply like to make an argument for (and provide a template for) the development of a full IMC plan. As such, let us look at the tactical executions available to entrepreneurs to enable them to attack and exploit their markets.

THE ADVERTISING PLAN

Advertising plan development is a comprehensive process of studying your targeted audience, identifying their needs and wants, and then developing an advertisement that speaks to that audience. Keep in mind that we often segment our markets, as discussed in chapter 1, and we may need to have more than one method of speaking to our audience(s). Once we understand the audience, we look at the media they consume. Different audiences enjoy different media, thus, as advertising professionals, we need to find the media that are most often utilized by the consumers in our target. Additionally, we have to speak to our audience in their language. A thorough understanding of the audience will increase your chances of advertising and business success.

As with all other areas in business, there is no one correct way to develop an advertising plan. In this chapter, we present one of the more common methods for plan development and provide a template you may use to facilitate your planning process. Now, let's begin.

Figure 4.1 gives an overview of the steps necessary to create an effective, synergistic, and integrated advertising plan. Although the development of advertising is sequential, it is also imperative that the plan be constantly updated, as changes in the business environment and universe will force you, the advertiser, to modify, and at times, drop certain elements of the campaign. This is a dynamic document that must be kept up-to-date, not a static piece.

Figure 4.1
Steps in an Advertising Plan

1. Executive Summary
2. The Situational Analysis

   History of the product/brand
   Brand and product review

Consumer information and profiles
Competitive review

3. Advertising and IMC Objectives
4. Total Budget Recommendation
5. The Advertising and IMC Plan

Restate the target market
Advertising objectives
The creative strategy

6. The Media Plan

The media problem
Objectives for the media
Media strategy

7. IMC Recommendations
   a. Advertising
   b. Branding
   c. Cybermarketing
   d. Direct marketing
   e. Personal selling
   f. Sales promotion
   g. Methods for generating publicity and carrying out public relations
8. Evaluative Techniques

Although no two advertising plans are the same, most include the aforementioned areas. Additionally, when you begin to develop your plan, we suggest the following:

1. Include a readable executive summary. Often, individuals, committees, providers of funding, and other audiences do not want to read through a 60-page plan, but would rather read through a comprehensive executive summary. Make your summary to the point.
2. Use the KISS Principle on your plan . . . *Keep It Simple, Stupid*. No one will read your plan to test your literary acumen. Rather, an advertising plan is written to communicate an entrepreneur's ideas and thoughts in a solid, clear, and consistent manner. Make the plan easy to read.
3. Advertising plans longer 60 pages will not be read. Instead of including a lot of verbiage in the plan, include graphs, charts, tables, illustrations, and other methods to break up the boredom of reading. Do not clutter the plan with too much detail.
4. Keep repetition to a minimum. If you covered information in one section (such as the target market profile) there is no need to repeat it; instead, refer the reader back to that section of the plan.
5. Include a reference list so that readers know where your information comes from. This adds value to your plan as you begin to execute it by providing outside expert advice to its development. References strengthen

the plan and allow you, as an entrepreneur, to become an expert in your area, about your competition, and concerning your industry.

6. Begin and end with the most important concepts. In other words, tell the reader what you are going to say, say it, and then tell the reader what you said in a summarization.

7. Use no Pronouns. No one cares who wrote the plan.

8. Make sure the plan is free of errors, as it may become one of your marketing tools.

9. Read and reread your plan. You may provide your advertising agency with your plan, and they must have an understanding of what you are really saying, but you must still reread the plan. Have your associates or employees read the plan and make comments. Make sure the plan outlines exactly what it is you think you should do.

Keeping these suggestions in mind, let's begin to develop your entrepreneurial advertising plan.

There is no perfect plan for any advertising campaign. You can, however, strive for perfection by including data and information that will be essential for the struggle to win additional sales. The more information and data you can collect prior to the creation of the plan and its execution, the more you will be able to reduce risk and ensure working dollars. Use the following steps should as a guide, but feel free to change, add, or omit sections of the plan that are not applicable to your business or industry.

The Executive Summary

An executive summary is one of the key sections of any advertising plan. Because ad plans can be as long as 50–60 pages, the executive summary allows you (or your employees), to see the entire outline of your campaign at a glance.

Although the executive summary will be the first item to appear in your plan, it will be the last item created. An executive summary provides an overview, or summarization, of the entire advertising campaign. Executive summaries should be well written, logical, to the point, and have a great sense of flow. An executive summary outlines the major areas and concepts of an entire plan. Begin and end your summary with the two or three plan elements that are most crucial for your success. Make sure all of the items speak to the reader and are understandable. Additionally, make sure to support, with research, all of your views and positions taken for the execution of the advertising campaign.

We recommend limiting your summary to no more than two pages.

The Situational Analysis

The situational analysis will allow you to generate research that will be used in the future, as you are beginning of the planning process. In turn, the analysis allows advertising planners to create a seamless, IMC campaign during the execution process. For the executive summary, become an archeologist and dig up all of the information and data about each of the topics listed below. The more data you can gather at the beginning of the process, the better. Once you have compiled all of the facts and information from those data, omit all unimportant or useless information and get down to the important facts for creating a research-base for the campaign/plan. Avoid a lot of unnecessary text by using graphs, charts, pictures, and other tools that get the point(s) across without relying too heavily on the written word.

We suggest keeping your situational analysis to around 10–15 pages. Below is a list of information, data, and facts we find essential in the creation of ad campaigns. Use those that apply to you and ignore those sections that do not. Keep in mind that all plans are different and need to be adapted and modified for your current objectives.

History of the Product/Brand

- What is the brand and/or product's background?
- What are the levels of budget support the brand/product has seen in the past?
- What have been the past advertising themes and why?
- What are the impacts of the technological and patent positions and history of your products/brands?
- What have been the past media expenditure patterns?
- SWOT (Strengths/Weaknesses/Opportunities/Threats) as they relate to the brand.
- List all relevant environments that may have an impact on the advertising of the brand/product (i.e., legal, technological, political, and social, etc.)
- What is the current creative theme?
- Accumulate all relevant marketing data from all previous and/or current marketing and advertising plans.
- What major events will occur during the campaign period that may have an impact on the advertising?

We suggest creating as many SWOT analyses and product/brand comparisons as possible. Use historical comparisons to learn how your brand is doing compared to other campaigns. Make sure you have a thorough understanding of the brand and product's history.

Brand and Product Review

Once you know the brand/product history, it is time to review the product or brand that will be the focus of the campaign. A thorough product analysis/review will help to give you a leg up on your competitors.

- How does your product compare to the competition in terms of its features and benefits? How is the consumer acceptance of the brand?
- What additions or deletions have you made during the past five years? Are there new markets? New product uses?

- What makes this product unique or different than what is currently being offered in the marketplace?
- Do consumers have problems with the product? If so, what are they? Can the problems be corrected?
- How do consumers perceive the product? That is, do they perceive it as new, old, high-tech, low-tech, modern, old-fashioned, and so on?
- Are the current users minimally satisfied with the product/service?
- What is the product's distribution? Is it exclusive? Selective? Intensive?
- How is the packaging perceived and received by consumers (both intermediaries and end-users)?
- What is the label's history?
- Are there any specific service problems?
- What type of equity does your brand name have? Can it be leveraged?

Although these are just suggestions, you will need the majority of this information later as you develop your advertising executions. Make sure to include all relevant data pertaining to your product/service offerings. It is essential that you understand how your products and services fit into the markets where you are involved. Also, make sure to highlight areas you feel are important to the success of the advertising campaign.

Consumer Information and Profiles

It is important to create an accurate picture of your customer base, as data you gather and generate that applies to your market is essential to the success of your campaign. Make sure you amass as much data related to your product/service users as possible. It is important to understand the products' users. In terms of data, the more the merrier. Begin building your customer profile by generating data in the following categories:

Demographics

Demographic data are important because most research companies and the federal, state, and local governments in your markets present data in a demographic format. A demographic profile generates a good base for a general understanding of the market. Key demographics include: occupation, marital status, household income, household head(s), race, ethnicity, age, educational levels of household members, and number of children in the household.

Demographic data are numbers that describe given populations. If you want to report on a particular demographic, make sure you identify it such as the age demographic, or the education demographic, for example. This helps readers to understand which pieces of data you are referencing.

Psychographics

Psychographic data refers to the lifestyles found in a consumer base; thus, psychographics could also refer to lifestyle analyses. SMRB (The Simmons

Report) and SRDS (Standard Rate and Data Service) *Lifestyle Market Analyst* are resources that offer a great deal of information about generating psychographic data. Additionally, VALS (values and lifestyles) data are useful for offering a good snapshot of what a market looks like. Do not forget to include any research you have already generated from past marketplace data related to your previous campaigns.

One of the best things about utilizing psychographic data is that it gives marketers the ability to target an audience directly. There are numerous media available to people, but marketers must choose the best media possible to reach their targets. Consequentially, having knowledge of the most typical lifestyles found in your customer base will help you to achieve this goal. For example, one of our clients sells "spring shoes," footwear developed to offer pain relief from foot, back, or leg pain. Not everyone would be interested in these products, however those individuals who are on their feet a lot might be interested. By understanding what the customer's lifestyles were, the company was able to identify nurses (and other health-affiliated occupations) as prime prospects for the shoes based upon their interests in holistic health, their lifestyle of standing during much of their workdays, their socializing habits, and their interests outside of work. These bits of information led the company to select outdoor and health-related media for the placement of their advertising messages.

Geographics

Geographic data tell *where* a market is. Recently, there has been a merger between demographic and geographic information creating a pool of data referred to as *geodemographics*. Often, geodemographic data are utilized in conjunction with geographical mapping software. We recommend exploring software programs such as *Simply Map* to earn more about this field. The merger of geographic and demographic data can help to generate a great picture of a given marketplace.

Behavioristics

Finally, it is important to understand how a consumer market behaves. The study of a market's behavior is called *behavioristics*. Useful behavioristic data includes information about influences on consumer consumption. In other words, where is the product used? How is it used? What are consumer attitudes toward the products' reputation, coloring, styling, and so on? What is the major problem the product is solving for consumers? Who influences the consumer's purchasing and shopping behavior? How do the consumers shop? CEO and researcher Paco Underhill, in his book *Why We Buy* (updated edition, 2008, published by Simon and Schuster), explains how different types of consumers shop at the point of purchase. He gives hints to the readers about how to merchandise and sell products at the point of sale. This is important because many sales are made at the point of purchase. The easier you make your customer's job of buying, the more they will buy and the happier they will be. Tom was part owner of a sporting goods retailer in Colorado. During every hunting season, Tom had a lot of traffic through his stores. Many of his customers, he discovered through a geographic analysis, came from Texas. Having an understanding of his customers' geography helped Tom to understand the customers' buying motives. As Tom dug deeper into information about his customer base, he found similarities about the customers' lifestyles and shopping behaviors. Tom responded to this information at the point of purchase. He know that his customers liked shopping for sporting goods products with a friend or alone, never with a spouse or significant other. Additionally, by watching how the shoppers came into the store, walked through it, and purchased products, Tom was able to rearrange the store to increase his sales. Tom noticed that his customers were reluctant to go toward the back of the store. Tom kept his fishing lures there and noticed they were not selling. By watching his customers' buying behavior, he was able to identify the problem of slow lure sales, move the lures to a dump table in the front of the stores, and increase his sales almost 300 percent. He was able to drive sales by understanding how his customers shopped his store.

An understanding of how your customers behave will be valuable when you begin to execute you advertising campaign.

After all of the information and data are collected, you should develop a "typical customer profile" outlining what your typical customers looks like. Who are they as people? We recommend that you name your typical customer market to provide guidance as you develop a communications campaign that satisfies (or wows) your customer base. Remember, the more you know about your market, the more successful you will be. A number of years back, we wanted our employees to feel and act like the customer group of one of our clients, the Dodge Neon. In order to get our employees thinking like the customers, we created a typical customer profile of the people who made up the market for the purchase of the cars. The result was a campaign based on Nick and Nancy with their Neons. Nancy Neon was typical of a customer who is in the market for a "Neon-type" vehicle. Our profile developed empathy for our customer base, new effective creatives were developed, and a campaign was born and launched.

Once your customer evaluation is complete, it is time to review your competitors. Again, the more you know about your competition, the better you will be able to build strategies and execute your advertising.

Competitive Review

Numerous data items are needed for a competitive review. We suggest that, at a minimum, you generate answers to the following questions:

- Who is our direct competition?
- Who is our indirect competition?
- What strengths do our competitors have in terms of advertising and IMC?

- What advertising and MARCOM themes have our competitors used over that past five years? Ten years?
- What are the strengths and weaknesses of competitive offerings? Conduct a competitive SWOT analysis.
- What are the competitive weaknesses you discovered in your SWOT that can be exploited?
- Other than advertising, what do our competitors do to promote and communicate their products and services? How successful are these activities? Would any of them lend themselves to our advertising or promotions? Is there any research that can verify competitive IMC effectiveness?
- List any data/information you can get in regard to competitive budgets and spending.
- What do our competitors' geographics look like? Are they the same as ours? How about their demographic, behavioristic, and psychographic data? Is there anything that stands out?
- How do their sales programs and plans compare with ours?
- Is there trade acceptance for competitive products and services? What does the trade like? Dislike?

There is no such thing as having too much data. Generate as much information as possible, and act on it. You should not just collect information . . . use it!

Once you have compiled all of the data and information, you will have a fantastic situational analysis and a great start for the development of the rest of your plan. After you have developed your situational analysis, it is time to focus on the development of your IMC and advertising objectives.

Advertising and IMC Objectives

An important and often overlooked section of the advertising plan is the development of sound objectives. It is important to know where you are going and how you are going to get there prior to departing on an excursion. This section may be the most important that you develop, as your objectives will be used at the end of the plan to assess how well your plan performed during the campaign period. Spend time and really think about what you want the campaign to accomplish.

Make sure that your objectives are stated so that they are measurable. Most of the time this means making your objectives quantitative, as opposed to qualitative. Numbers are easily tracked, and increases (or decreases) in sales and profits can easily be measured. Additionally, make sure that your objectives have a time period included so at the end of the campaign, you may tack the campaign's effectiveness for any given period of time. This will allow you to make effective, positive changes to your campaign as it unfolds.

Budget

Your campaign budget will depend on a number of factors. For entrepreneurs, cash is almost always an issue. The better your advertising plan, the more effective and productive your monetary investment in your advertising will be. Budgets should be developed and based upon campaign outcomes. It is for this reason that we recommend using an objective-and-task budgeting system.

With objective-and-task budgeting, you need to make a wish list of what objectives your campaign should achieve. This step is fairly painless, as you developed your objectives in the prior step. With your objectives in hand, create a list of executions, or tasks that need to be performed in order to reach the objective. Once the tasks have been identified, all you need to do is generate costs that will be associated with each of the tasks. Adding the costs together will give you an overall budget.

We recommend you begin your budgeting process by trying to include all necessary tasks or executions. Generate a total monetary amount needed to achieve the goals and objectives. Once you know the total advertising costs, adjust your plan accordingly. That is, if the budget amount is too high, eliminate or delete your least effective objectives. If the budget amount is too low, add more tasks and tactics to help you achieve your objectives. Finally, if the budget is just right, move on to the creation of your advertising and marketing communications plan.

The Advertising and Integrated Marketing Communications (IMC) Plan

One of the last steps in the development of your advertising plan is the creation of its IMC portion. All of the hard, labor-intensive work has been completed. In this section of your plan, the idea is to create an overall picture of what the communication vehicle integration will look like. As such, it is best to start by condensing and restating some of the facts you have already dug up.

Begin by restating your target market so that you will have this information in the forefront of your mind. Though we did tell you not to duplicate your sections previously, this is an exception to the rule . . . always keep your customers at the top of your mind when involved in advertising, so restate what you already know, your target market. We also recommend that you include your typical customer profile(s) in this section.

The second step is to identify and restate your objectives. In this section, your objectives should relate to and reflect the work that you want your tactics to perform. For example, public relations (PR) builds brands, while advertising sustains them. Knowing this, you may have a PR objective that deals with reaching as much of the audience as possible (quantify this using numbers or percentages), while your advertising objective may deal with the development of frequency for the target market. Regardless, the point is that each of the controllable variables (the IMC/advertising tactical executions) has specific strengths and weaknesses. Your use of the tactics should be objectives-based and predicated upon what you want your communications to achieve.

Finally, you need to develop and insert your creative strategy. We will provide additional information on how this is developed in chapter 7, which that discusses the crafting of the message. Creatives should guide not only the advertising portion of your plan, but also the other IMC variables executions. Thus, the creative strategy will guide the creative executions and is very important. Often, all three tasks, as outlined above, can be included within the creative strategy. The creative strategy is also referred to as the creative position, or the copy platform. We recommend, at a minimum, including the following bits of information in your creative strategy:

1. Review your target market and target audiences
2. State your advertising objectives
3. List your creative strategy and copy platform

The Media Plan

One of the most important decisions in the development of your advertising campaign is the media you select to carry your message. Each medium has a unique audience, so an understanding of the audience is essential. Thus, in this portion of the plan you need to lay out your media program as completely, yet also as briefly as possible. It is important to include descriptive information about the market and the various audiences of the media vehicles from which you are choosing. Include all information that will be relative to your plan. You will need to include the *media problem, media objective,* and *media strategy.* The subject of media planning is somewhat complex, so we will cover media in greater depth in chapters 5 and 6. For now, we simply want to show you where your media plan will fit into the larger advertising and IMC plan.

What is the key media problem? In other words, what specific problem or issue will the media plan solve? The advertising message that you plan to communicate to your audience must be the correct message being communicated to the correct people (i.e., your customers).

What are your media objectives? What, specifically, do you hope to achieve from the media plan? Relate your media to your overall marketing and IMC plan. Make sure it is integrated. Since we are developing objectives at this point, make sure your statements are measurable and quantifiable. Generate data based upon the following:

- How is the target audience(s) best reached in terms of the four "-ics" (demographics, geographics, psychographics, and behavioristics)?
- What is the available budget? Are there any budget restrictions on the use of media?
- What is your frequency objective?
- What is your reach objective?
- What type of continuity are you trying to generate? How will it be created?
- Are there any geographic restrictions? Which geographic areas offer the most potential? It may be a good idea at this point to create some impor-

tant indexes such as the CDI (Category Development Index) and the BDI (Brand Development Index) in order to create a picture of your geographical market area.

- What will be the impact of the other nonadvertising creative executions (i.e., PR/publicity, cybermarketing, sales promotion, branding, personal selling, and direct marketing efforts)?
- What are the media implications for the creative strategy?
- Will the media have to support other promotional activities?

We suggest developing and listing a rationale for each media decision you make. This will help to support your plan.

Once you have developed your key media problem and media objectives, it is time to create your media strategy. The media strategy covers the specific executions involved with the media plan. Because of this, you need to list each of the media you are proposing to use, and for each of those media, you need to provide information and data supporting why that particular medium was chosen. It is wise to link each of your media strategies to your media objectives, thus making it easier to evaluate the effectiveness of the media plan as you execute the advertising.

Media strategy development is difficult; so do not be afraid to ask for assistance from friends, family, colleagues, professors, consultants, media firms, advertising agencies, or any other person who may have some insight into the selection of media. Keep in mind that if you leave it up to professionals involved in the media industry, they will steer you toward their products (i.e., television reps will try to sell you TV, radio reps sell radio time, newspaper reps sell newspaper space, etc.).

In order to execute your media plan, you, as an entrepreneur, will have to do a bit of homework to generate answers to the following questions. The preceding chapters have provided you with many sources of information you will want to access to help answer these important questions. As you develop your media strategies, we recommend that you include, at the minimum, the following:

- Which media classes are you selecting and why (i.e., television, radio, magazines, newspapers, outdoor, etc.)?
- What strategy will you use for resource allocation?
- How will you allocate your capital resources toward each of the media classes? (Include both a dollar number and percentage.)
- Include a rationale for each strategy you list.
- Is there a relationship between your strategy and your competitors? If so, explain the relationship (especially when you are dealing with key brands).
- Include a flighting plan with recommendations. What basis or criteria will you use for selecting and scheduling your media?
- Specify what media units you want to utilize (i.e., 15-second, 20-second, 30-second spots, full page ads, fractional page ads, three months of billboards, etc.).

- How will you weight your media markets?
- What is the cost-per-thousand (CPM) for the ads?
- What are the GRPs (gross rating points)?
- What are your total exposures?
- Are there secondary markets that need to be reached? If so, tell how you will reach them and what budget amounts will be necessary.
- Include your reach and frequency levels needed for the year, quarters, and four-week periods.

When you have completed your strategy development, it is time to move on to finishing your media plan. If you know what your media plan looks like, you can apply your tactics to the plan and execute it. The next section of this chapter looks at the various controllable variables available to an advertising entrepreneur (i.e., the tactics).

The Integrated Marketing Communications Variables (IMC Tactics)

When you are developing the tactical executions for an IMC plan, there are a number of variables that you can control. These variables are referred to as the IMC, or MARCOM (Marketing Communication), mix.

While advertising forms the base for the plan, other variables will be used at different times during the campaign to stimulate traffic into stores or other points of service, change consumer perceptions, and encourage product trials to increase sales and enhance other objectives. The variables included within the IMC mix help each other in terms of achieving the plan's objectives.

IMC mix variables include the following:

- Advertising
- Branding
- Cybermarketing
- Direct marketing
- Personal selling
- Sales promotion
- Publicity and public relations

Advertising. Advertising is the process of communicating to the market in an impersonal manner, utilizing some form of media and identifying the company or organization placing the ad as the sponsor.

Branding. What is the strength of your brand? How much equity is in the brand's name? Is the brand reflected in the logo? The brand serves as a silent salesperson allowing our customers to differentiate your brand from the product offerings of competitors. Since the brand communicates, it is best developed within the advertising venue.

Cybermarketing. Any advertising or communications done using the Internet, databases, or other forms of technology delivery are referred to as "cybermarketing." Online ads, computer game placements, DVDs, videos, database marketing, and customer relationship marketing (or CRM), as well as other types of advertising, are used as tactical executions within this area.

Direct marketing. Direct marketing is used to stimulate immediate and measurable sales. It can utilize any form of media, as long as the message is looking for an immediate customer action. Couponing is one of the most frequently used direct marketing methods. Additionally, direct mail, telemarketing, infomercials, and radio pleas are also among the tactics used in direct marketing.

Personal selling. Personal selling is direct, face-to-face selling. It typically occurs when an organization or business is involved in business-to-business (B2B) marketing, but is also be important in retail sales.

Sales promotion. Sales promotion activities are used to stimulate sales. The sales stimulation often occurs at the point of sale, but may also appear elsewhere. Sales promotion activities are meant to help support other areas of the IMC mix. Business cards, pens, pencils, point-of-purchase advertising, sweepstakes, contests, and other types of business gifts are forms of sales promotion.

Publicity and public relations. Publicity and public relations are used to create a positive image of a product, brand, company, organization, or some other idea or concept. Publicity is not controllable, so it must be used carefully. The primary advantage of utilizing PR and publicity is that it creates a third-party endorsement of your product, store, organization, and so on. Again, publicity is uncontrollable, so often business owners generate positive as well as negative publicity. There is a saying in advertising that goes something like this: "Public relations and publicity build a brand, advertising sustains it." With this in mind, is best to create a strong PR campaign toward the beginning of product or campaign launches, and then transition the IMC executions to more of an advertising base.

Once the tactics are in place, the plan can be executed. Make sure that someone manages the plan as the executions appear in each market. Additionally, the plan must be evaluated and controlled to make sure it is the most cost-effective, yet ambitious plan available. The final section of this chapter deals with the issues of evaluation and control.

Evaluative Techniques

Include a statement within the plan indicating how the overall plan, and its sections, will be evaluated. Any proposed methods of research should be also covered in this statement. Although there are many formal techniques for advertising evaluation, the most popular is to look at sales numbers.

Smart entrepreneurs look at the objectives that they have set. If you go back to your objectives for each of the sections and for the overall plan, you will be able to generate a good idea of how well you did with your advertising budget. We have our clients create a method of assessing the ROAI (return on advertising investments); this allows them the luxury of deleting from the advertising campaign those things that do not work. Additionally, a reevaluation gives plan executors a chance to change geographic allocations as needed.

On important nuance to recognize is that the environment in which an entrepreneur operates will have an impact on advertising effectiveness. If there are
uncontrollable variables in the environment (i.e., a worsening economy, war,
inflation, deflation, political changes, technological changes, or legal changes,
to name a few), for example, the entrepreneur needs to take these into account
when assessing the effectiveness of a plan. Oftentimes, it can appear that an
IMC was not effective (based upon sales) when, in fact, it was.

Now that you are an expert on advertising and IMC planning, use the following outline to think through your plans. Use each item as a heading under
which you can fill in the blanks with information and data to help you to
become successful.

1. The Executive Summary
   Place your executive summary here. It should be the last section of the
      plan written, but placed at the beginning of the plan.
2. The Situational Analysis

   a. History of the product/brand
   b. Brand and product review
   c. Consumer information and profiles
   d. Competitive review

3. Advertising and IMC Objectives
4. Total Budget Recommendation
5. The Advertising and IMC Plan

   a. Restate the target market
   b. Advertising objectives
   c. The creative strategy

6. The Media Plan

   a. The media problem
   b. Objectives for the media
   c. Media strategy

7. IMC Recommendations

   a. Advertising
   b. Branding
   c. Cybermarketing
   d. Direct marketing
   e. Personal selling
   f. Sales promotion
   g. Methods of publicity and public relations

8. Evaluative Techniques

This chapter dealt with issues in the development of an advertising plan.
Specifically, it addressed:

- The function of IMC
- The advertising plan
- A fill in the blanks template for an entire plan has been provided.

Chapter 5 deals with media basics, and will be a starting point for an understanding of what media is and how it effects you as an entrepreneur.

SUMMARY

- ☑ Your IMC effort, like your marketing plan, is planned, executed, and evaluated often.
- ☑ Keep your advertising plan simple, to no more than 60 pages, and do not be repetitive.
- ☑ Your advertising plan is a synergistic, integrated, and dynamic document that should continuously be referred back to, monitored, and changed to reflect any changes in your business.
- ☑ Stick to your overall advertising objectives. Straying from them will likely mean that you are misallocating your budget or running the risk of not reaching your target market effectively.

Media Basics

This examines the world of media as the primary means for conveying advertised messages. It discusses which factors entrepreneurs need to pay attention to in order to select media and what to watch for when it comes to timing, geography, and other factors. The goal of this chapter is to give you the knowledge to put together the most effective media mix, and, in turn, a media plan, to reach your potential customers.

WHAT IS MEDIA?

The word "media" can conjure up a lot of scary images for entrepreneurs, from the evening news anchors delivering shocking stories to exorbitant half-time commercials during the Super Bowl. In fact, working with the media should be anything but scary. Think of the media, first and foremost, as a collection of mediums. These mediums are simply the means you will employ to deliver your message to your target audience.

Often referred to as media "vehicles" or media "channels," these means come in a variety of sizes and shapes, or, more importantly, come in a variety of places and times. It is likely that you already come into contact with many forms of media as you go about your daily activities. The more traditional media vehicles include television, radio, newspaper, magazines, and outdoor or out of home coverage. Some media experts will argue that online advertising has now become one of the more traditional media as well. This chapter will focus primarily on these media, but will also touch a bit on some of the more nontraditional forms of media a little later.

WHAT IS A MEDIA MIX?

As the introduction to this chapter suggested, the goal at this point is to put together an effective media mix. The media mix that an entrepreneur puts in place is no more than the select combination of media in which advertising is placed. While logic will tell you "the more you place, the more people will hear or see your message," you need to ensure that you reduce risk (and waste) while maximizing efficiency and effectiveness. In order to do this, you need to know what all of your options are.

Think of a media mix like a recipe and the different mediums as the ingredients. Your mix of these mediums (such as radio, billboards, and newspaper) and the amount of each you use will develop your overall media plan. Much like the advertising plan in chapter 4, there is no perfect media plan, yet there are many *correct* possibilities for your media plan, just like there are many combinations of flour, eggs, sugar, and other ingredients that can be used to make cookies. If you add cinnamon, the cookies will taste different than if you add vanilla. Similarly, if you add television to your media mix, your media plan comes out differently than if you were to focus solely on print ads.

WHAT ARE THE OPTIONS WHEN IT COMES TO MEDIA?

You might say to yourself, "I want my advertisements to be everywhere, all the time, for everyone to see and hear." In essence, you are saying that you want your mix to include *everything*. Wouldn't this be the best way to get the most customers?

Realistically, we know that advertising is something one must pay for, as mentioned in chapter 1. Unless you have an unlimited budget, you will be limited in where you can place your message and how often, or to what extent, you can place it. We will talk about budgets at the end of this chapter, but for now it is important for every entrepreneur to know that budgeting can be one of the biggest factors in choosing the selected media or inclusion in the media mix.

Let's look more closely at the traditional options:

1. Print (i.e., numerous periodicals including newspapers, magazines, tabloids, organizational publications, directories, playbills)
2. Broadcast (a.k.a., Electronic) (radio, television)
3. Out-of-Home (billboard, transit, bus shelters)
4. Online (banner and block ads, video pre-roll, pay-per-click links, paid positioning Search Engine Optimization)

To give you a clear picture of how these forms of media differ, let's look at the pros and cons of each:

Print

Newspapers

Pros:
- Newspapers have a good reach and high circulation.
- Newspapers have longevity as a trusted tool for information delivery with high acceptance and credibility.
- There is a very short lead-time for placing and providing advertising, which means that messages can be timely and updated quickly.
- Newspapers are a good vehicle for couponing and inserts.
- They are accommodating when it comes to the size and shape of advertising, with many new customizable and attention-getting options available.
- Different sections allow for demographic targeting.

Cons:

- Newspapers may be viewed as information overload and are often cluttered.
- Newspapers offer little in the way of exclusivity or competitive protection.
- Rates are increasing for ad space.
- Many markets across the United States have multiple papers servicing the same geographic areas, creating crossover and occasionally complete duplication.
- Newspapers are a passive medium, making it difficult to force the reader to act.
- Many newspapers are struggling with subscription and newsstand sales due to the online presence of similar news content and their own electronic versions being available.

Magazines

Pros:

- Magazines offer a very targeted readership and often cater to a special interest or particular demographic.
- Content can often be targeted regionally, even in some national consumer magazines. Magazines offer good geographic selectivity in larger markets (city by city).
- Most magazines tend to be printed on high quality, glossy paper, keeping photos crisp and clean, which helps the look of your advertising.
- Ideal for image and branding campaigns.
- Many magazines have a long shelf life and exceptional pass-along value. Some are even collected or highly coveted.
- Now, more than ever, magazines are offering unique advertising spaces and technologies to those advertisers who really want to cut through the clutter, such as stickers, pre-printed inserts, pop-ups, fold-outs, and the like.

Cons:

- Ad space costs are increasing.
- Frequency can be limiting, as you must wait month to month, or longer to change a message.
- Magazines tend to reach a relatively low percentage of their overall target market.
- Magazines tends to have a high ratio of ads to editorial content.
- Readership is low in comparison to other media. Only three percent of people's leisure time spent engaging with media is spent reading magazines.
- The increase of online information and e-zines has slightly decreased the need for print versions.
- The lead time for placing an ad and preparing the copy/ad mechanical is well in advance of the publication date.

Broadcast

Television

Pros:
- Television is used by more people, and for longer durations of time, than any other medium.
- Reach is very good.
- Television has a high impact.
- A good choice for image and branding ads or campaigns.
- A story can be told, and multiple variations of a spot can be created, thus different selling messages can also be conveyed.
- There are few restrictions on creativity.
- Particular times of day can be targeted.
- Ad rates are relatively low considering the amount of reach.
- Inventory availability tends to be high.
- There is a growing presence of a viral marketing aspect to television ads, as more and more television programs and ads are shown online, especially via social Web sites and video content sites such as YouTube and Hulu.

Cons:
- The cost per thousand impressions (CPM) is high for television.
- Recall of television advertising tends to require a higher frequency than other media.
- It is simple for a viewer to avoid advertising by "zipping and zapping," or skipping and surfing, during commercials.
- Production costs are high.
- Viewing, in general, has seasonality to it, and tends to drop at certain times of the year, such as the summer months.
- Technology now allows viewers to record programming without commercials.

Radio

Pros:
- Reach is good on radio, and frequency is easily maximized.
- Radio is somewhat geographically targeted.
- There is a low CPM.
- Advertising is flexible, and can be changed relatively quickly.
- Advertising remains locally relevant, as it is heard only in a select market.
- Allows for a longer, more elaborate message to be conveyed.
- Production can be kept relatively inexpensive.
- Particular times of day can be targets.

Cons:
- Like television, listeners can move away from a commercial to another station, missing the message entirely.
- Radio is a passive medium, as most listeners are engaged in another activity while listening, thus some distraction can occur.

- Radio stations, while catering to specific types of listeners, overlap significantly with each other within a market; therefore, you may find it necessary to buy ads on multiple stations in order to fully deliver your message.
- Different times of day can deliver very different types of listeners, even on a single station.

Out-of-Home

Outdoor

Pros:
- Based on CPMs (or cost-per-thousand), outdoor advertising has a relatively low cost.
- Advertising tends to be large and more in your face, resulting in greater impact than many other media.
- One can target geographically quite well with this approach, down to the specific neighborhoods where billboards will be displayed.
- Simple ads can be the most effective.
- Ads can occasionally include other technology that draws attention, such as temperature or time.
- Advances in outdoor displays have opened up all sorts of possibilities, from the popular tri-vision or tri-wave boards, which change messages in five- to eight-second intervals, to attention-getting digital displays, which are as vibrant as most television screens.

Cons:
- Ad messages must be brief.
- Effectiveness and total reach are relative to traffic flow and weather.
- Image can be impacted by the location's immediate surroundings.
- Recall of billboard advertising tends to be low.
- Space, or inventory, can be limited in many markets.
- Changing a message or correcting an error in an ad can be costly.
- Only so much can be said in the allotted space.

Online

Pros:
- The message can be changed easily.
- Online advertising is easily engaged.
- The cost of advertising, whether it is based on CPM, cost-per-click, or some other gauge, is relatively low.
- The number of people spending time online increases dramatically each year.
- Demographic, psychographic, and geographic targeting is possible based on the highly specific nature of most Web sites.

Cons:
- There are millions of Web sites to choose from.
- Measurability and effectiveness are more in question with online advertising than any other medium.

- You are responsible for paying close attention to click-throughs, hits, and the resulting actions taken by the viewers. (However, online behavior is more trackable now than ever.)
- Most people online are not there for the advertising, thus many view it as intrusive.

WHAT FACTORS AFFECT MY SELECTION OF MEDIA?

As mentioned before, an entrepreneur's advertising budget (which is a portion of the overall marketing budget) can be one of the biggest factors in deciding which media to utilize to convey your message. It is not the only factor, however. Below are other important considerations when putting together your media mix: target market, relative geography, competitors, timing/seasonality, and your message.

The Target Market

Probably the single most important exercise you will find yourself engaged in, as an entrepreneur, is defining your target market, and it is a process will be repeated often, as you dissect your potential customer base from various aspects. For some entrepreneurs, the target market has been defined since day one because the product or service they are creating is catering to fills an obvious need or void. Most entrepreneurs' great new product or service must be purchased by someone, and it is up to them to define who that someone is.

Now it is time to define your target market as it relates to media. The potential customers have not changed, but you must pay attention to attributes that align themselves with the audiences of different media. These attributes are more commonly referred to as demographics and psychographics. As we define these attributes again, try to think about them as they relate to both your target market and the audience who is watching, hearing, or reading an advertisement. It is this process of finding that person who is both the audience of the media and a member of your target market that will determine your media selections.

Demographics are the characteristics of a group of people, or more specifically a segment of the population, as defined by age, gender, ethnicity, occupation, marital status, household income, education level, or some other feature.

Psychographics are characteristics that relate to the activities, lifestyles, behaviors, and attitudes of a group of people. Examples of psychographic characteristics are "drives an SUV," "enjoys golfing for pleasure," and "eats out two to three times per week."

All media options should make available to you details about the audience they deliver, in the form of demographic and psychographic information. It is up to you, or an outsourced partner such as an advertising agency, to play the matching game and determine the media outlet that delivers the greatest amount of your target market for your budget.

There may come a time, as you watch your customer base grow and take shape, when you begin to identify segments within your target market that have unique qualities to them, or better yet, can be reached through a highly targeted selection of niche media. It may be that a portion of your target market has a particular background or interest, or perhaps a portion of your target market identifies with and partakes in a particular lifestyle. One good example is the evolution of a popular lunch and dinner spot in downtown Allentown, Pennsylvania. The high-end grill and cigar bar, with stylish décor and eclectic American/South American fare, became popular with gay and lesbian patrons, so much so that the owner was encouraged, by her patrons and her advertising agency, to run ads in an up-and-coming magazine in the region, called *Gaydar,* which celebrates people of all sexual orientations. The advertising, while containing messages that spoke specifically to the gay, lesbian, and bisexual customer base, was consistent in look and feel with other ads placed in more mainstream media outlets. This is an example of how a customer base can dictate which media an entrepreneur will select.

Another example is when a portion of your potential customer base shows loyalty to one business versus another, in order to intentionally differentiate themselves from the rest of your target market. Take, for instance, a small college town with pizza shops lining the main streets. What dictates the fact that one pizza shop is the most popular place to grab a slice if you are an athlete? Or that another is a better hangout for freshmen and sophomores. Maybe this is based on word-of-mouth, or maybe tradition, but one thing is certain: the customers are telling *owners* who they are and what they want, not the other way around. As a pizza shop owner, your hope is to cater to all students at the school, giving you the best chance for success and the most sales, but your customer base is dictating otherwise. This could easily affect what media you choose in order to reach more customers.

Relative Geography (Coverage and Distribution)

As you consider who your target market is, you must evaluate the places from which your potential customer receives his information. This may relate most closely to where he lives, so it would be a good idea to look at what media reaches customers in their homes. Or, it may be more relative to him during his commute to and from work, so out-of-home options might be the best.

Be sure to not overlook the fact that media that has only a local or regional reach can be a limiting factor. For broadcast purposes, it would be the coverage area in which the radio signal can be picked up or the system that carries a particular television network. For print, it would be the area of distribution. Remember, geographically speaking, the exposure of your advertisement is only as vast as the medium itself. You may also have to consider not only the area covered by the medium, but also the driving distance that your customer is willing to travel or the locations in which your target customers reside.

Competitors

An old adage advises "Keep your friends close and your enemies closer." This applies in business as much as it does in war. Always keep a watchful eye on what your competition is doing and where they are placing their advertising. It will leave you with two choices when it comes to placing your own media. "Do I go up against their message within the same media, or do I approach my target through a means that is underutilized by my competition?" The answer will depend on how much of a foothold your competition already has, the aggressiveness with which they are advertising, and the strength, or angle, of their message.

Timing and Seasonality

You should consider whether or not there is something about your product or service that warrants your customer realizing their need at a particular time of day, or during a particular season of the year. Plenty of businesses have an obvious seasonality to them, from lawn and garden stores to ski resorts, and some businesses cater to customers differently as the day goes on, not unlike a restaurant changing its menu from breakfast to lunch to dinner. Keep in mind that timing within your media placements should be sensitive to when your customer is making her decision just as much as when she takes advantage of your product or service. For instance, reminding someone that you are open 24 hours per day may be best conveyed during the 9 to 5 workday when you can reach her with an e-mail letting her know that she can stop by later, at her convenience.

Your Message

Finally, you will have to examine the pros and cons of each medium to determine which will deliver your message in its most beneficial form. Does your product or service have qualities or features that translate better across one medium than another? For instance, making a viewer's mouth water for gourmet ice cream or specialty brick-oven pizza may be easier to do with great visuals on television, than by trying to explain over the radio how good it is, or perhaps the use of sounds on radio (like the sound of a Little League ballgame, for instance) can more easily transport an adult back to his childhood than that of a photo in a print campaign. Ask yourself, "Which media deliver the best emotional triggers?" and "Which media will help my potential customer to understand my product or service the best?"

HOW MUCH SHOULD I BUDGET FOR MEDIA EXPENSES?

Think of advertising not as a cost, but as an investment. Like any good investment, there is a return on the money spent that should supersede the original investment. Sometimes the return is easily seen, such as "heads in beds" for the hotel owner, or inventory flying off the shelf if you make and sell a product. These different types of returns affect your bottom line in a rather short time period, relatively speaking. Sometimes, however, the return can be a bit more intangible. While you need your business to be profitable, never discount those elements that are less measurable, such as building brand awareness and brand loyalty. As a general rule of thumb, many businesses designate about 80 percent of their total marketing budget for media placements. That being said, this number can be significantly lower for start-ups or those businesses that are creating a new or different advertising campaign, as production costs may be greater.

Perhaps the better question to ask yourself is, "How much can I afford to spend?" If you ask yourself this before selecting media, it will save you from having to rework your media mix down the road, after learning that your plan may cost more than you have available. It is possible, however, to put a media plan together that, in turn, dictates back to you what your media budget should be, and if you have done the work to define your market and select the best media vehicles, you should be able to trust that your plan will deliver your message to a relevant audience with little waste or risk. You may then decide that the execution of the media plan is worthwhile, no matter what the investment.

MAXIMIZING YOUR RETURN

There are a number of possible options to consider when planning and placing media that can help you, as an entrepreneur, to save money. Some of these considerations may not apply to your type of business, and some cases are more relevant to a start-up business than one that has been operating and advertising for some time, but all are worth learning about.

1. Are *co-op dollars* available to you from any of your suppliers or business partners? For instance, if you are operating a nail salon, is there a line of polish that you use which would offer to pay for a portion of your advertising costs simply in exchange for you mentioning their name or placing their logo in your advertising? Similarly, there may be a neighboring business (ideally one with a similar target market) that would be willing to split the cost of advertising with you to share an ad space, in a *cooperative effort*. This can be most effective when the creative execution of the ad focuses on the synergy between the benefits of each entity, thus providing an even greater benefit back to the listener, viewer, or reader. For example, a pizza shop and ice cream parlor may split a full-page ad in a coupon magazine, each taking a half page, thus conveying the message of dinner and dessert in one stop.
2. *Contract rates* (bulk-inch or annual investment)—When placing media, always consider what your entire commitment will entail and ask your representative if there is any savings associated with signing a contract outlining the entire buy. Newspapers, for instance, often make a lower rate available to those advertisers who are willing to commit to a certain number of column inches within one year, or a certain level of dollar investment for a year. For other media, such as radio, it is simply better to lock in a campaign for its entire duration in order to secure the best rates up-front.
3. *Frequency rates*—Many media outlets will provide a lower rate for advertisers willing to commit to a number of placements up-front, versus placing

ads one at a time. The best example is monthly magazines, which often offer a 3-time rate, 6-time rate, and 12-time rate (or something similar) for advertisers willing to commit to more than one month at a time.

4. *Added value*—Always ask your representative what she can offer, in addition to the actual schedule you are placing, to help increase the frequency with which you are mentioned. Many publications, especially trade or consumer magazines, can offer some editorial coverage surrounding your business, products, or services, especially if it is highly relevant to their readers.

5. *New advertiser advantages*—As an entrepreneur with a new product or service, your business will need all the help it can get, but being the new guy on the block has its advantages too. Ask your media contact or representative what he can offer you, in recognition of your status as a first-time advertiser. Perhaps he can secure for you a premium position in a publication at no additional charge, or *gratis* spots during overnight times on radio or television.

6. *Grandfathered rates*—There are advantages to be had by becoming a continuous advertiser, such as asking your representative to honor the rates to which you have become accustomed, versus any increases. This can be especially helpful if your marketing budget does not increase from one year to the next.

7. *Nonprofit / charitable rates*—Though most entrepreneurial businesses do not operate as nonprofit entities, those that do, given their federal tax status which identifies their tax exempt nature (such as a 501(c)3), may be able to take advantage of special rates or deals from the media. Please note that often, with nonprofit media space, there are exceptions or limitations placed upon the type or size of space made available.

8. *Trade agreements*—If you have a product or service that you are willing to offer to the media in exchange for free advertising space or time you should definitely keep doing this in mind. Not every medium will be inclined to take you up on your offer, but some may, at least for a portion of your advertising investment. Some media, such as radio stations, welcome the idea of getting gift certificates or gift cards that they can, in turn, use as incentives for their listeners, and the added on-air mentions that you receive during the giveaways and promotions can be priceless.

9. *Sponsorships*—Occasionally a media company may agree to be a sponsor of an event or activity in which your business is participating as a promotional effort, such as an in-store celebrity appearance, a book signing, or a sweepstakes or give-away. In turn, this could result in donated ad space or time in that medium as part of the sponsorship agreement.

10. *Use of an agency or media buying service*—As an entrepreneur, you have many things to worry about when it comes to the success of your business. Consider putting the task of media planning and buying in the hands of someone who does it all the time. You may find that savings you enjoy are far greater than the fees charged by these companies, mostly because they are placing larger amounts of advertising, perhaps on their own bulk contracts, through representatives with which they have long-standing relationships.

RECAP

As you can see, the subject of media is a complicated one. We have attempted to write an easy to understand chapter dealing with the use of media and simplifying some of the tougher concepts. The coverage of media basics allows us to develop additional, more in-depth coverage of media that will be presented in chapter 6. In particular, we will show you how to put your media plan together with your newfound media knowledge. Once the media portion of your IMC plan is complete, you can begin your task of executing the plan and making sure that it is integrated into the other areas of MARCOM.

Specifically, this chapter covered issues related to:

- What media are
- How to create a media mix
- The pros and cons of media selection
- The factors that impact the selection of media
- The media budget
- How to maximize media investment.

SUMMARY

☑ Do not let media get the best of you. It can be intimidating at first, but if you approach your media placements like a buy from any other supplier, a relationship with the media should emerge, making your job even easier.

☑ When aligning your target market with specific media options, do not just consider who your potential customer is, but where they are, what they using to gather news and information, and when they are tuning in.

☑ All forms of media have their pros and cons, and it will be your task to decipher when one is a better option than another. When it comes to mass media, all forms deliver some reach and frequency, but it is also be your job to maximize the return on your investment.

☑ When it comes to setting aside a budget for media expenditures, be creative! Think about how to save money through other value-driven interactions with the media, such as sponsorships, co-op dollars, and in-kind trade. These can all result in added media exposure with little or no actual cash outlay.

6

Choosing and Executing
Your Media Plan

This chapter takes the different forms of media discussed in chapter 5 and puts them together as your media mix, but within the constraints of a desired timeframe, within your proposed budget, and with set ad sizes and shapes. This expanded version of your media mix is your media plan. The chapter also discusses flighting, pulsing, reach, frequency, and other media terminology that you are sure to come across as you execute your media plan and place or run your ads.

TURNING YOUR MEDIA MIX INTO YOUR MEDIA PLAN

As the introduction suggests, your *media plan* is an expanded version of your media mix, during which you can begin to make media selections based on the pros and cons outlined in chapter 5. Like putting words together with a tune to create a song, we will now examine how to create a schedule for your media mix to create the overall media plan.

The other role of your media plan is to elaborate on the size and shape of your advertising, the length of television or radio spots, the position of your print advertising, and/or the size and location of your outdoor advertising. The media plan will outline the timeframes for each medium and the specific ads or messages that should appear in each form of media. Your media plan will be your guideline all throughout your advertising campaign and can be referred to at any time so that you know exactly what ads are running and where.

THE SIZE AND SHAPE OF ADVERTISING

In order to plan your media placements, you will need to understand what is available to you when it comes to ad sizes and shapes within each medium. As you are probably aware, or are now finding out, advertising comes in an endless number of sizes and shapes, from the modular sizes of magazine ads to pixel dimensions of Web page ads, from half-hour infomercials to five-second sound bytes on radio. To help narrow your options, this chapter highlights some of the more common sizes and shapes that you can expect to come across, broken down by medium.

In print advertising, you are faced with selecting the most appropriate or affordable dimensions for your advertising, based on the sizes made available by the publication. It is possible that, while you would like to do the largest ad possible, such as a full-color, two-page spread ad in a lifestyle magazine, your budget may only allow for a half-page ad. Your budget may also dictate that you must make a size selection in order to get a certain amount of frequency. For example, within the same budget you may be able to do three consecutive issues of full-page ads, but in an attempt to make the campaign extend over a longer time period, you may opt to run six consecutive issues of half-page ads instead. It is also possible that your creative approach may require a certain amount of space in order to be executed properly. For instance, if a zoo is running an ad for a new giraffe exhibit, it may be a vertical-shaped ad design (for obvious reasons). Therefore, the visual works best when used in a half-page vertical ad space in the magazine, and a full-page ad is not necessary.

Common magazine ad sizes include two-page spreads, full page, two-thirds page, half page (vertical or horizontal), quarter page, one-third page (vertical and square), and one-eighth page. It is not uncommon for magazines to allow one-sixteenth page ads, although this size is typically reserved for restaurant listings or other special grouping sections. Some magazines also offer a half-page island ad, which normally covers two-thirds of the page in width, but not quite the entire height of the page, so editorial or other advertising fall to the side of the ad and above or below the ad. Some special opportunities in magazines include, but are not limited to, pages with an extra fold-out section, pages of a heavier paper weight, stitched-in or bound-in response cards, and tipped-on (or glued-on) stickers on the cover.

Newspapers, like magazines, also base their ad space on dimensions or portions of a page, however, rather than the inches wide by inches high, the space within a newspaper is referred to as column inch space. The formula for figuring out your ad size is to multiply the number of columns wide that you would like the ad (most papers' pages are six columns wide) by the number of inches high, up to a full page in height, or approximately 20.5" for most papers. For example, if your ad covers 3 columns in width, and is 10 inches in height, your ad size is 3 columns by 10 inches, or 30 column inches. This is important to understand, as newspaper ad space is often contracted based on total column inches. Additionally, more and more newspapers are making the move to a standardized set of ad sizes. These modular sizes dictated by the paper include full page, half page, quarter page, one-eighth page, and others, and all ads must match one of the set sizes. By this standard, pages of the paper can be laid out in a more manageable fashion, much like a magazine. Something else to keep in mind when placing ads in multiple newspapers is that all newspapers do not have the same column widths, therefore one single ad may need to be resized numerous times in preparing the material to be sent out.

When it comes to grand scale, few options beat out the ever-popular vinyl billboard, or bulletin, as they are also known. The most typical of size of a large billboard, but far from the largest, is 14 feet high by 48 feet wide. There are many other sizes and shapes of billboards, but this size has remained the most common for a number of reasons. For one, the material produced for use on this size of billboard is a printed vinyl, with a lifespan of anywhere from three to five years, or even longer. The more times you can reuse the vinyl, the better the investment. Billboard companies often encourage the moving around of your vinyl, cycle after cycle, in order to deliver your message to an entire market over time. This type of program is known as a *rotary bulletin,* since the location rotates through a set number of boards. This only works if all boards in the rotary program are the same size.

In outdoor advertising, the whole idea is get attention. Sometimes getting attention means delivering a number of messages, or *impressions,* across a more widespread area of coverage. In this case, outdoor advertising also comes in the form of a *poster panel.* Poster panels, or poster billboards, get their name from the fact that the material in many markets is still a set of paper, adhered side-by-side in order to create the entire image. The typical size for poster panels is 12 feet high by 24 feet wide. One benefit to using this type of billboard is that the structures are often smaller, so they can be placed on secondary roads, in neighborhoods, or smaller communities. Geographically speaking, you can spread your message across an area a bit easier with a number of poster panels, as opposed to a single, large bulletin.

Other means of outdoor advertising offer a variety of their own corresponding shapes and sizes. Transit advertising has many forms, and if you think about a bus ride or ride on the subway, it makes a lot of sense. There is plenty of empty space to place an ad, and best of all, you have a captive audience for the length of their commute. Bus shelters offer large, poster sized advertising, both inside and outside, which can often be illuminated or backlit at night. Similarly, there are often opportunities throughout bus and subway stations to place advertising, often in the form of a poster or banner, and even video more recently in some cities. Buses and subways themselves offer ad space or boards inside, for passengers, and outside for other drivers and onlookers. With sizes often referred to as queen, king, or double-king, these boards, or panels, appear on the sides, front, and back of the bus. The more aggressive of advertisers have even wrapped entire buses with their advertisements, which are see-through from the inside looking outside.

Perhaps the Goliath of all outdoor advertising, when it comes to size, is the building banner. While it is not media *per se,* unless a media company has brokered the space, it is a form of outdoor advertising and is worth mentioning here as it relates to billboards. With the only limits being cost, and possibly fastening capabilities, the wall-hung banner, also known as a wallscape, has grown to enormous proportions and recognition. Once only considered for messages such as commercial and residential real estate for sale or lease, and only seen in large cities, the vehicle has now taken on a life of its own. More affordable now than ever, thanks to large-format digital printers, banners can be hung (with permission, of course) from train trestles, bridges, and buildings, creating a presence that is larger than life.

Like the video screens and scrolling message in Times Square, there are plenty of great examples of outdoor advertising that may not be so typical in your town. Think about how you can adapt some uncommon style of outdoor advertising within your market.

Relatively easy ad formats to talk about when it comes to size and shape, television commercials do not stray too far from the most frequently seen 30-second spots. However, in some markets, or better yet on some networks or across some cable systems, television spots of different lengths are allowed, such as 60-second spots, and even 15-second spots. One technique often employed by advertisers such as Geico and McDonald's is to utilize multiple 15-second spots within the same commercial break, either back-to-back or separated by another advertiser's spot; this practice is known as using *book-end spots*. This works best when the brand is highly recognized and the message remains simple. Other less common ad shapes on television include the tagged promotional spot and lengthier infomercial. A tagged spot will usually include a logo for a few seconds and mention your company as a supporter or sponsor in conjunction with a special program or show that will air on a particular channel. An infomercial can take on a length anywhere from two minutes to one hour, though anything lasting more than a few minutes may require you to let the viewer know that it is an advertisement or paid programming they are viewing and not a television show.

Radio, like television, has a limited number of options when it comes to the length of ads; however, there are some options that are worth inquiring about when speaking with your sales representative. In addition to the normal 30-second and 60-second radio spots, the 15-second spot is becoming more and more common. Especially since younger generations have become more accustomed to receiving their information in quicker, smaller doses. Listeners are also distracted more easily now than ever before, and not only has our attention span been shortened, but in a situation like driving in the car, we are bombarded with multiple messages all competing for our attention. Unless a spot is highly informative or engaging, it may be better to go shorter. Recognizing this fact, Clear Channel Radio tested and made a 1-second to 5-second spot available beginning in 2006. Referred to as a *blink*, these extremely quick sound bytes often combine a recognized jingle or theme song with a quick sentence. One of the first to take advantage of this quick, unique format was FOX in its promotion of premiers that year for *24*, *Prison Break, House,* and *The Simpsons.*

An example of a blink might be something like the highly recognizable McDonald's jingle, "Doodoot doot doot doo . . . I'm lovin' it!" or an ad for Mini Cooper, in which you simply hear "*Beep. Beep.* Mini!"

Radio also offers a sponsorship style of mention, in which the advertiser pays to have their business mentioned before, during, or after radio content such as traffic updates, news, weather, sports, and so on.

The sizes and shapes of advertising now available on the Internet are as vast as one's imagination. In fact, the more unique the shape, the better your chance of being seen and remembered in most cases. One thing to remember when considering Web site advertising is that people are usually online for information or a particular activity. The key is not necessarily the size of the ad, but more importantly its timing and keeping it from being annoying. Give people a reason to look at your ad and engage it. Once you have them clicking on your ad, there are no boundaries to size except for the screen, and even scrolling can overcome that limitation.

Typical online ad spaces are across the top of a Web page, in what is known as a banner ad or leaderboard, or in the form of a box, or block, somewhere on the page. Tall boxes that span the side of a screen are called skyscrapers. Some boxes, especially leaderboards, can be made to expand larger automatically, allowing the viewer to engage the ad like a mini Web page, but always with the option to be closed by the viewer.

While online advertising remained static for nearly its first decade of existence, now it is anything but. In fact, static banner and block ads are easily overlooked, as they call no attention to themselves. Luckily, technology devoted to the creation of advertising has kept pace with the advancements in online content. Static ads have become animated and are no longer contained in a defined space on the page. Now, when a Web site has a video player on its page, the space or time before the video starts can be sold to advertisers, in the form of pre-roll video, usually a 10- to 15-second commercial. Even banner and block advertising now allows video to be embedded within them.

The key to understanding the sizes and shapes available to you is spending time with your potential media options. Again, put yourself in your target market's shoes and see the media the way they see it.

WHEN AND WHERE?

Now that we have discussed the sizes and shapes available to you within each medium, the matters of when and where are considerably less complicated.

Print advertising can be as simple as choosing a magazine issue to start running in, or a start date to begin an ad schedule in newspaper. Just remember what we said earlier about the lead-time needed when placing certain advertisements, such as magazine ads, which may have deadlines two to three months before the issue actually hits the streets. When placing ads in daily newspapers, make sure you get a full media kit from your sales representative outlining when certain sections come out during the week. Not all sections of a newspaper come out every day. For instance, a section focused on the home or health may appear only twice a week, and a section focused on arts and leisure, or weekend activities, may only come out once per week, on a Thursday or Friday. This type of section may be of particular interest if your entrepreneurial business is a restaurant or leisure/family activity.

When placing print advertising in a magazine or newspaper, it is always a good practice to request "far forward" and "right read" placement. Like it sounds, this request will put you towards the beginning of a publication and on the right-hand page. Obviously, it is impossible for everyone to be far forward and right read, but it never hurts to ask. For some publications. you can expect their frequent or contracted advertisers to get preferential treatment, and for other publications, reserving a specific location means paying a premium price, or at least an additional fee.

There are times when you may not be as concerned with being far forward and on a right-hand page. This is especially true when the content is consistently read throughout, the articles are well written, and/or the publication is held onto as a resource or reference piece with a longer shelf life than other publications. There may also be times when you specifically request to be near a certain article, or in a particular section of the newspaper. By knowing to whom you are directing your message, you may find it better to run your ad in the sports section (with a higher young male readership) than the health section (with a higher older female readership).

The daily schedules of television and radio are both broken down into what are called *dayparts*, and you will select when you want your ads to run based on your preference for time of day, particular programming, or the rate associated with each breakdown of a daypart. For instance, on radio, many advertisers have a strong preference for their spots to air during A.M. and P.M. drive times, some of the most heavily listened to times of the day. Likewise, on television many advertisers prefer to hit viewers during the weekdays and in the evening hours, also known as *primetime*. While this is when most viewers are tuning in, it also comes with a more premium price tag. In fact, the tighter you choose to narrow your daypart on radio or television, the more likely you are to increase the cost per spot, so much so that the highest-priced spots on television are often program-specific placements, or *fixed-position*, meaning you are choosing a particular show, and possibly even a particular commercial break, during which your ad will air.

To balance out the more expensively placed spots on both television and radio, many advertisers choose to compliment these fixed-position spots with a number of spots placed in a more open daypart. These placements can occur any time within a specified timeframe such as Noon to 4pm, a more open timeframe such as 6 A.M. to 6 P.M., and the most open and often most cost-efficient, a 24-hour ROS. In this case, *ROS* stands for run-of-station or run-of-schedule, meaning any programming at any time would be suitable.

In addition to daypart options on television, you also have options when it comes to which networks you choose for your advertisements. If you are placing advertising on local cable systems, contact a sales representative at the cable network and ask for demographic information about the viewers of each channel they offer, or better yet, describe to the representative who your ideal target market is and allow them to make recommendations of a balanced mix of cable channels. Your selection of cable channels could differ greatly just based on sex, age, or household income level of your target market.

As for online advertising, the when and where decision has a lot more to do with which Web sites are relevant to your business and your target market. Web sites that offer a lot of advertising within their pages often sell ad space on subsequent pages based on the relevance of the content. For instance, if you look at your local newspaper's Web site, you will notice that the homepage is appropriate for any advertiser, since the content is nonspecific, but it on a subsequent page, such as the online health section, you may find more ads for orthopedic specialists, nursing homes, and fitness clubs because they know they will be in front of someone already predisposed to think about their health. Some Web sites can now offer you specific dayparts during which your ad will run, similar to those on television and radio, however, since the demographics of the visitor are unlikely to change as drastically as television, and there is more uncertainty as to when your potential customer actually accesses a Web site, dayparting your online ads may not be of much interest.

Finally, your own business may dictate the timing of your advertising. Is your advertising leading up to an event or special promotion? Is there a specific timeframe during which your advertising is relevant or valid? Do your offers have an expiration date? Does your advertising, or better yet your product/service, have seasonality to it? Is there one time of year that makes more sense to advertise than another?

LOCAL VS. REGIONAL VS. NATIONAL ADVERTISING

Geographically speaking, you will also have to make a judgment call on just how far you expect to draw your customers from. Is there a willingness to travel a great distance to get your products, or is there a limited geographic area that you are servicing? Perhaps, thanks to telephone, catalog, and online ordering capabilities of your business, there is little in the way of geographic boundaries affecting your market. Still, you will have to how far you hope to spread your message. *Local advertising* takes place when your message is placed throughout a single market. This market can be as small as one town, or as large as a cluster of neighboring towns or cities. Individual markets across the United States have been labeled, by Nielsen Media Research, as Designated Market Area (DMAs). Some are metropolitan areas with one city at its center, such as New York City or Philadelphia. Others have a number of neighboring towns and cities pulled together to form a single DMA, such as the Harrisburg-Lebanon-Lancaster-York, Pennsylvania DMA. These DMAs, of which there are 210 across the country, are most often used when referring to television audience calculations. Radio markets have similar geographic breakdowns, however they tend to be smaller than DMAs and based on the reach of their own AM or FM broadcast signal. The FCC also has a description of these television market areas, known as Television Market Areas (TMA).

Regional advertising can refer to a large, single market, often including a large city and its surrounding suburbs. It can also refer to a grouping of multiple DMAs, states, or portions of states. The major difference between local and regional advertising, from a media standpoint, is that regional advertising requires far more individual buys to be made, based on the coverage of each medium. For instance, with regional advertising, you increase your likelihood of having multiple cable systems, multiple radio stations within the same format, and multiple local publications in which to place ads. All of these media vehicles will have to be brought together in your plan in order to fully encompass the region that you are trying to reach.

National advertising, just as it sounds, is a much wider, often coast-to-coast, for of media buying. Advertising this way comes with a price, but of course it is all relative to the size of the market and number of people you are trying to attract. The good news is that, if your advertising would require a full-blown national effort, there are agencies and media buying firms that can make these buys on your behalf, lumping all of the individual DMAs or other markets together into one cost-saving placement.

HOW MUCH OF EACH MEDIUM SHOULD I USE?

In order to decide how much of each medium to put into your media plan, you need to look at each one separately and ask yourself, and your sales representative, "What size of a buy will be an effective one?" This is a delicate balance, of course, as too little will run the risk of not being seen or heard, and too much may be a waste of your money. Others will argue that, until you have reached market *saturation* with your message, which is the point at which your message is no longer seen or heard no matter how often the market comes in contact with it, you cannot advertise too much and that sales should simply grow exponentially with every additional spot aired or ad placed.

Of course, you do not have an unlimited budget, so some decision of how much to buy is always the case. In fact, it is probably more of a question of "What percent of your budget should be allocated to one medium versus another?" That, in turn, will dictate the amount you can invest. We recommend starting with the investments that have a firm or fixed price to them, such as a magazine ad. This is not to say that you cannot negotiate with your representative, but in the end, the cost of the ad is firm, compared to something like radio where you can adjust your overall buy by a few spots in order to adjust your costs. One approach is to figure out what you want to do in print, online, and outdoors initially, if they are part of your mix, and then look at the more flexible investments of radio and/or television. You can always revisit print, online, and outdoor and make further adjustments to your investment if you find that you have not reserved enough for radio or television.

Deciding on an amount to invest in a particular medium is somewhat subjective and can also differ from market to market, as one form of media may get a better response in one city than another. When it comes to the effectiveness of a media buy, keep in mind that, for your business specifically, the message in your advertising can also affect the effectiveness of the media plan if the effectiveness is based on sales, phone calls, or some other tracking mechanism. We will talk about tracking and measurability a little later in this chapter.

You will probably find yourself re-shaping your media plan over time, trying new things and eliminating those media with which you had little response. Trial and error is normal for any business putting an advertising plan in place for the first time, but in order to reduce the risk and wasted dollars as much as possible, there are other generalized gauges of effectiveness with which your sales representative from each media vehicle can help you. While there are many terms for the different measurements and calculations, the most commonly used are *reach, frequency, GRPs,* and *CPM.*

Reach is the number of individuals (or in some cases, households) who have seen or heard an advertisement at least one time. In most cases, reach is expressed as a percentage of the overall population. Keep in mind that, while your ad has a certain percentage of reach provided by a particular medium, that medium may only reach a certain percentage of the geographic areas population itself. Reach is also an unduplicated count of the audience.

Frequency refers to the number of times that an individual (or in some cases, a household) has seen or heard an advertisement and is typically expressed in terms of average number of times per month.

GRPs (or *Gross Rating Points*), like reach, show a calculation of the total number of exposures of individuals to your advertising. In the case of GRPs, however, the totals are derived from *all* exposures, meaning there is audience duplication. The simplest way to arrive at your GRPs is to multiply the average reach times the frequency that each of those individuals sees or hears your ad.

Therefore, reach multiplied by frequency = GRP.

> Example: Sixty percent of the population is reached by your radio spot an average of 4.5 times in one month ($60 \times 4.5 = 270$). Your GRPs for that station is 270.

A similar calculation can be done for each medium if your sales representative can provide the average reach and frequency, and then a comparison can be done from one medium to the next to show what delivers the highest number of GRPs, and, in a sense, delivers the highest number of gross impressions and greatest exposure.

Because you must formulate your media plan before you can actually obtain your real reach and frequency figures, you must rely on the historical averages provided by each medium and calculate your expected GRPs. To ensure accuracy with the reach of media, some research companies such as Nielsen (for television) and Arbitron (for radio) have taken on the task of recording the number of listeners and viewers and established a ratings system for each program, show, or daypart. These *ratings* reflect the percentage of the population exposed to a single airing of a show or a single daypart, and therefore they can be substituted for the reach of a single ad on that show or within that daypart.

CPM (or *Cost Per Thousand*) is another effective way to compare your media mix selections, in that it is derived by taking your total investment in a medium divided by the number of total viewers or listeners who come in contact with the ad or schedule (in thousands). This calculation gives you a comparable figure for each different media investment based on the cost to reach 1,000 people with each.

Therefore, the cost of the advertisement divided by the number of contacts (in thousands) = CPM.

> Example: A single full-page ad in a local lifestyle magazine costs you $3,000 and the circulation is 25,000 ($3,000 ÷ 25 = 120). Your CPM is $120; it costs $120 to reach 1,000 people with that magazine.

If it costs $140 to reach 1,000 people with a similar publication in the market, the magazine in the example above would be a better investment (i.e., more bang for the buck), and if you are forced to choose one over the other, the CPM is one gauge you can use. It is important to realize, however, that many other factors, and not just the CPM, may play a role in helping you to make that choice. Radio, for instance, may have a much lower CPM than local cable, and yet the ads on television are providing a function that radio cannot deliver.

Another thing to keep in mind when using CPM to make a comparison between two media options is to make sure that you are comparing the same reach numbers. For example, if one radio station has a CPM calculated using the total percentage reached of a geographic area's population and a second radio station has a CPM calculated using the percentage reached of a specific demographic, such as females aged 25–54, you will get a significantly higher CPM for the second radio station. This could be seriously misleading, since you are not comparing apples to apples.

Ultimately, it will be up to you to decide what the best reach and frequency are for your advertising. It could all depend on the type of product you are introducing and the amount of educating that you will need to do through your ads in order to make a sale. The more complicated a product is to understand, the more frequency you may need to convey your full message. On the other hand, the simpler the product, the easier it may be for an individual to understand his need for it, and therefore a greater reach could be put in place, knowing that it takes less convincing for one individual to take the initiative to get in touch or make a purchase.

LENGTH OF CAMPAIGN

Another personally subjective call, the overall length of your campaign, is up to you. However, when laying out your media plan, there are a few key things to keep in mind regarding the amount of time for which you intend to run or air your ads. Here are some general pointers:

- Repetition in advertising is often key to generating good recall and a valid response, since it can be difficult to judge the effectiveness of an ad after just one or two appearances. This is especially true if it is solely a branding ad or has little call to action. This may sound like common sense, but all too often advertisers are quick to evaluate an ad or campaign that has just begun to run or air and do not allow it to get enough frequency with the target market to be effective.

- Committing to multiple ads in a schedule at the same time often allows a sales representative to offer some form of frequency discount; therefore, the further out you can project that you will be placing ads, the better off you will be from a budget standpoint.
- Outlining a schedule of ads over the course of weeks or months can eliminate the nuisance of constantly having to deal with deadlines and ensures that ads are not accidentally missed.
- Advertising campaigns have a life to them. They begin at some point and end at some point. (Of course, we can all probably name a campaign or two that felt like it ran for an eternity.) Pay attention to what your competition and other local advertisers are doing in the way of campaign duration. This could provide a guideline for how long your ads will need to be present in the market. Recall of an ad is likely to be better if the ad has been viewed or heard more recently. If a similar business has ads running after your campaign ends (media selection, reach, and frequency being similar), there is a good chance that their product or service will be more top-of-mind than yours at that point in time unless, of course, your ad content is more memorable (in a positive way).

BUDGET

Though chapter 5 has already touched on your media budget, this is a good time to mention a few additional budgeting suggestions as they relate to the media plan.

A famous quote, which has been variously credited to Lord Leverhulme, John Wanamaker, and F. W. Woolworth goes something like this: "Half the money I spend on advertising is wasted; the trouble is I don't know which half." The truth is, this is a terrible position to be in, feeling that you are wasting your money somehow or somewhere. While many advertisers half-jokingly feel this way all of the time, it is important for you to feel comfortable with your media plan in order to execute it effectively; you need to know that you have done everything you could to this point so that you can trust what you are about to put in place. Once your advertising schedule or campaign is set in motion, you should watch it closely, as it is now the voice of your business; it is out there, creating impressions, intrigue, and generating inquiries. The worst things you can do, however, are to sit back, cross your fingers, and forget about your media plan. Media plans are always malleable and can be revisited at any time. Some media placements, more easily than others, can also be cancelled, postponed, repositioned, or reallocated as you see fit.

WHEN AND HOW TO PLACE YOUR ADVERTISING

Placing media should be an enjoyable process (or at least an easy one), as long as you stay on top of deadlines and consider all of your options. Like making cookies, media placement is where the batter hits the pan. All the work you have done to this point should reinforce that you have selected the correct media.

Unfortunately, timing can dictate that it is now or never for some media. Deadlines, such as when a magazine goes to print, can often cause an advertiser to make a rash decision, or media representatives can put you in a yes or no situation for which you may be unprepared. Every media placement you make will have a specific lead-time relative to that medium. Advertising in some mediums, like radio, can be put on the air within hours, if the airtime is available and the spot is already produced or in the can. Advertising in other mediums, such as magazines, needs to be placed well in advance of the publication date, often months earlier. The materials (or files) for the advertisement must also be in the hands of the publication on or around this deadline. You will often hear the commitment deadline referred to as the "space deadline" and the deadline for receiving files as the "materials deadline." These binding commitments, which often happen months in advance, can create headaches and even problems if you are not careful. On the upside, the earlier you can make your space commitments, the better your exposure could be, such as a better position in a publication or a daypart on radio or television with more listeners or viewers.

This is why it is important to plan your advertising far enough in advance to ensure that you have allowed enough time to not rush the placement when the time comes, and also to ensure that you are taking advantage of discounts or premium space availability before other advertisers. Your *media plan* is a critical tool for helping to keep an eye on these deadlines. We will discuss the visual appearance of your media plan, also called a *flight plan*, in more depth later. (Please note that allowing plenty of time is just as important in the creative development of your advertising, which we discuss in chapter 7.)

As for making the actual ad placement, the process can be as simple as making a phone call to the respective media company, for which contact information should be easy to track down in phone books and local business directories, or better yet, online or within the medium itself (remember, magazines and other publications always have contact information listed within the first few pages). When you first make contact, ask for an advertising sales representative. You may be asked to describe your type of business and/or location so that you can be assigned the most appropriate associate for your needs. One thing to keep in mind, as a business owner, is that your interaction with your media representatives should be treated as a relationship, not unlike any good buyer/supplier relationship. The more you know about that media company and the more the representative knows about your business, the better off both parties will be, and especially you as the advertiser. Early on, as each side is learning how the other side operates, it will be important for you to know that the representative is sharing as much information about placements and opportunities as possible; likewise, it will be important for her to know that you are serious about your placements and committed to a successful advertising effort.

Insertion Orders vs. Contract Agreements

Commitments for media space can take on a number of forms. Ad placements and space reservations made directly with an advertising sales representative typically happen in one of two forms, as an insertion order or a contact agreement. While the purpose is virtually the same thing, to secure your advertising space or time with that media company, and both are contractually binding, the look and content can be a bit different. Here is a description of each:

An *insertion order* is an advertising placement typically drafted by the advertiser, or an agency, on behalf of the advertiser. It would be sent to the attention of the representative and has all of the pertinent contact information for the person and business placing the ad, as well as specifications and information specific to the ad, such as the headline of the ad or name of the spot, size or length, dates or issues, position or dayparts, and costs. After emailing or faxing your insertion order, it is a good practice to follow up with your representative, if he has not confirmed receipt of the order, which may also be referred to as an "I.O." By doing this, the costs can be confirmed and you will know that your commitment is in place. Furthermore, even though an I.O. is a binding contract, some representatives prefer to follow up your order with their own version of a contract. There are also instances when you can verbally or less formally request your placement, and the representative will draft his own version of an insertion order for you to sign.

A *contract agreement*, as mentioned earlier, is put in place for the same reasons that an insertion order is created, to commit you to advertising space, but is normally drafted by the media company. While the contract agreement will include most of the same information specific to the ad that the I.O. has, you will be provided with more information specific to that medium. For instance, a radio or television contract will often have the ratings, reach, frequency, and GRPs noted, and outdoor contracts will often show Daily Effective Circulation (often referred to as DECs), another term for impressions, and also give specific specifications about each billboard location, such as the direction it faces and whether or not it is illuminated at night.

Another important aspect of the contracts drafted by the media company is that they may outline what your overall commitment during a campaign or a set timeframe will entail. For instance, a magazine contract may outline the fact that you are committing upfront to every monthly issue for a year, earning you a "12x" contract level rate because you are placing it all upfront. This would be considered a *frequency contract*. A newspaper contract may state that you are committing to a certain number of column inches per month or per year, known as a *bulk inch contract*, or perhaps that you are committing to a certain level of dollar investment for the year, known as a *dollar volume contract*. Putting these types of contracts in place when you commit to your advertising will provide you with an up-front savings and may also afford you the opportunity to do more within the same budget. Just remember that, once in place, you must complete the ads to which you have committed. In some instances, a representative may allow you to cancel a contract, but you could also run the risk of being *short-rated*, or forced to pay for the difference in what a lower level commitment would have cost for the ads or space that you did complete.

If you are a first-time advertiser with a particular media company, it is not uncommon for them to request that you fill out a *credit application*, just as some of your other suppliers or vendors may do. The credit application simply supplies them with your bank information and references so that they can trust that you will pay your invoices. This is quite normal. Of course, because of all the contracts, information and ad specifications, ad materials, and invoicing that transpires between an advertiser and its arsenal of media outlets, it may be beneficial to look to outsourcing this portion of your business as well, to a media buying service, or better yet, an advertising agency.

YOUR MEDIA PLAN TAKES FLIGHT

Putting your media plan down on paper is easiest when it is laid out in a spreadsheet format, also referred to as a *flight plan*. This is because the different media being used, all listed in a column down the left side of the spreadsheet, have corresponding blocks of time (or flights) when they are running that appear as you move across the spreadsheet, which is also laid out with a row at the top showing a running calendar of months and weeks. It is up to you to decide how much of the calendar you want to show (i.e., 6 months or 12 months), but it is recommended that you break each month into columns of weeks, corresponding with a Sunday or Monday start date. (While typical calendars have Sunday as the first day of the week, keep in mind that most broadcast/media calendars start with Monday.) See the *example of a media plan* on the following page.

Below is a list of what you will want to make sure that you list or note in some way on your media plan:

- Specific media vehicles (i.e., publication names, types of billboard or outdoor ads, Web sites, cable systems and channels, radio stations)
- Details relevant to each ad in that medium (i.e., the size of the ad, day and section of paper, daypart(s) for spots)
- Start dates and stop dates for each placement (blocked out on the spreadsheet—it is often a good idea to color code these for easier reading)
- Titles or headlines of specific creative to run (if known, remember you can continuously add to and update this document) Another approach would be to simply list the areas of your business or special seasonal focuses across a row at the top of the spreadsheet (but beneath the calendar dates) which will outline the focus of your campaign at any given time of the year (for instance, if you are a lawn and garden store, your ads for summer furniture may take place from mid-March through mid-June).

Other details that could be added, depending on what is known and how extensive you want your details to be, are:

Figure 6.1
Sample Media Flight Plan

Floral Designs, Inc., Q1 and Q2 of 2009, Campaign Media Plan *(current as of Jan 09)*

	January	February	March	April	May	June
	5 12 19 26	2 9 16 23	2 9 16 23 30	6 13 20 27	4 11 18 25	1 8 15 22 29

Lifestyle Magazine A — Home ad, Full Page / Mother's Day ad, Full Page

Lifestyle Magazine B — Home ad, Full Page / Mother's Day ad, Full Page (2x)

Local Newspaper — Ongoing Sales Ad with Coupon, Sunday, Section A, 2 col. x 6" b&w ad

Outdoor
Rotary Bulletin — Big Flowers ad, 14' x 48' vinyl / Big Flowers ad, 14' x 48' vinyl

Poster Campaign — Big Flowers ad, 12' x 24', 12 posters

Local Cable — 0:30 spot "Big Flowers", FOOD, TLC, Lifetime, We

Radio Station A
Radio Station B — 0:60 spot "Big Flowers" plus weather sponsorships

- Cost totals (per media type and totaled)
- Reach, frequency, and GRPs
- Representative names and contact numbers (this is not a bad place to list this information for convenience, if you have the space)
- Other relevant dates (to keep all of your sales promotions, direct mail efforts. or even anniversaries in focus, as they relate to your media placements, and in order to assure continuity and consistency).

There are various techniques for the scheduling of ad placements, and through the visual of the media plan, we will be able to explain these different techniques and explain why each is used. The first is the *big splash* technique. Employed most often by new businesses advertising for the first time, or by a business advertising a new product or service, the big splash calls for running a schedule that has the largest portion of the media investment in the early part of the schedule, also known as *front-loading.* Sometimes described to as "coming out of the gates strong," the heavy up-front investment is done to ensure that your message is less likely to be missed, because you only get one chance to make a big first impression. Following a big splash, most advertisers will then employ a *maintenance* technique to keep the same message present in the market for a good duration of time, with a lighter, continuous investment.

Advertisers often put this type of even, continuous investment in place for entire campaigns from start to finish that run a relatively long time, are not specific to the launch of a new product, and have no time sensitivity to them. This technique is known as *continuous scheduling.*

Sometimes, however, your budget may dictate that a continuous schedule, no matter how light, is simply not practical, or, timing issues, as we have discussed before, may dictate that you need to have a stronger advertising presence at certain times of the year. For these reasons, you may look to employ a *flighting* technique, whereby your advertising runs for a set time period, followed by a period of no advertising, after which your advertising begins again. This can be an effective means of conserving dollars for the more important time periods and strengthening your presence when it will have the greatest impact. Your target market will notice when you are advertising, but often it takes some time for them to realize when you are not, the assumption being that they simply are not seeing your ads, but that they are out there.

Pulsing is a similar technique to flighting, except that it calls for a decreased advertising expenditure, rather than none at all. This can be a more comfortable technique for new advertisers, since it is a way to conserve some of the advertising budget while maintaining some presence in the market, rather than disappearing completely. There can be a temptation, when running flights of advertising, to take a longer break than planned, or, more detrimentally, not go back to advertising at all.

Regardless of the technique you choose, it is important to remember that your messages should be complimentary from medium to medium, unless you have a good reason to run different messages, such as multiple campaigns running simultaneously. Even more important to remember in this instance is that all of your advertising is acting as your voice, constantly reinforcing your image and your brand. For this reason, once mapped out in calendar form, your media plan should help you to identify synergistic opportunities and ways that one medium can actually refer to another. Remember, many drivers are listening to the radio as they pass dozens of billboards, and these same drivers will, at some point, go online or pick up a newspaper. It may sound odd to attempt to connect one medium to another, but how often have you heard "Check out our flyer in this Sunday's paper!" There is also a need for continuity across your other marketing efforts, such as sales promotions, direct mail, and public relations. Chapter 8 will expand on this in greater detail.

NONTRADITIONAL MEDIA

While a traditional media plan is, of course, one of the best ways to deliver your advertising and marketing message, it is not the only approach available to you. Never overlook the more unconventional means for advertising your brand or product. These alternatives, often referred to as *nontraditional media,* come in all shapes and sizes, places, and times. In fact, there is an endless world of nontraditional media available to you. It is simply up to you to find, or create it, and put it to work for you.

What do we mean by *create it*? The beauty of advertising in a nontraditional way is that it can happen anywhere you make it happen, legally of course, and depending on your budget. For instance, if your entrepreneurial business is a smoothie bar at the beach, believe it or not, there is a company that will custom-cut logos and/or messages into the bottoms of flip-flops. Now, every time you, your staff, or a team of "brand champions" walks the beach, you will have left tiny trail-like ads running up and down the sand. Best of all, you will have positioned your business in front of your potential customers at the time when they may need you the most. Not large enough? Depending on the size of the investment you are willing to make, there is another company that will drive a mini steamroller-like vehicle, with a larger engraved message, up and down the sandy shores of your customer-teeming target area, imprinting a seemingly endless amount of logos or messages into the sand.

Nontraditional media does not have to be off-the-wall or bizarre to work. In fact, it is often the simplest of ideas that gets the most attention and cuts through the clutter. Good examples are door hangers left across neighborhoods within a delivery zone or flyers placed under windshield wipers at a concert or sporting event. From skywriting to the backs of grocery store receipts, and from cinema slides to mall kiosks, there are few places that people have not placed ads, yet there is a good chance, given your entrepreneurial spirit, that you may just create the newest form of nontraditional media.

It is important to keep in mind when using nontraditional advertising, however, that it often should not be depended upon as your sole means of getting your message out. Nontraditional approaches typically function best when added to a traditional media plan for extra exposure, garnering attention for its uniqueness.

RECAP

Chapter 6 continued the discussion of pesky media issues. In particular, it brought together all of the concepts and theories available to create an overall media plan. The concept of media planning was covered, as was the importance of media to the IMC plan. Issues related to both traditional media and nontraditional media were discussed. Information on how and when to buy media was presented. Why buying too much of any particular medium was looked at, and the chapter concluded with a look at creating a budget for media buys.

Important and specific areas coverage of this chapter included the following:

- How to create a media plan
- The size and shape of media
- When and where to advertise
- How much of each medium to utilize
- The correct length for advertising and media campaigns
- Media budgeting
- When and how to place advertising
- The use of nontraditional media and why it is important to the entrepreneur.

The first six chapters of this book have focused on planning a campaign. The next chapter discusses the importance associated with the development of the communications message you want your target audience to be aware of. As you shall see, the value of messaging and the creation of your message are crucial steps in the development of effective advertising for entrepreneurs.

SUMMARY

- ☑ Your media plan will be your guideline all throughout your advertising campaign and can be referred to at any time so that you know exactly what ads are running and where.
- ☑ Talk with your media representatives about what you hope to accomplish with your advertising. They can often make recommendations on size, shape, and frequency to help you out.
- ☑ Watch media deadlines (for space and materials) very closely.
- ☑ To save money, commit to as much of your plan as possible up-front, and take advantage of frequency and volume discounts.
- ☑ Your media plan is malleable and should be monitored and reshaped when necessary.
- ☑ If you are a new business, or you are launching a new product, you only get one chance to make a great first impression. If this is true for you and your entrepreneurial business, keep the big splash technique in mind when putting your plan together and making your media buys.
- ☑ Never overlook the less obvious, nontraditional means for communicating your message.

7

Crafting Your Message

This chapter discusses steps to help you develop the content of your advertising, from the wording, or copy and the visual, to the call to action and necessary musts of the ad. The chapter also looks at different approaches to advertising creative and when to use each approach. It will also give you the tools to craft the particular message you hope to convey and discuss the response you hope to obtain from your target audience. Finally, it touches on the elements that go into making an ad and to whom you can turn for assistance with the creative process.

GREAT IDEAS ARE PLENTIFUL

You may be thinking, "I've had a great idea for an ad ever since I thought about starting my business." The truth is . . . that is quite common. We all see ads every day. We know which ads get our attention, and which will trigger certain emotions in us. Therefore, it is reasonable and justifiable to believe that you could take a lifetime of experience and interaction and apply it to the creation of your own advertising. In fact, there is nothing wrong with coming up with ideas for advertising early and on an ongoing basis, just be sure to take the extra steps we are about to outline when working with each potential ad idea to help increase your chances of obtaining the results you desire with your advertising.

Everything we have discussed to this point about branding, media, and advertising plans will lend itself to crafting the most effective advertising. It is not enough for your creative approach to be interesting, amusing, or hard-hitting, it must also be strategically sound. Your *creative strategy*, which will come out of your creative brief, is the fact-based approach that you and everyone involved (such as copywriters and art directors) will follow in order to create your advertising. This strategy will ensure consistency, help to keep your communications on target, and minimize risk and wasted time, effort, and money. Beginning by outlining specific facts in the creative brief process, which we will discuss shortly, will ensure that you are putting your best message and creative foot forward.

Any advertising that you may have thought about prior this point should still be compared to your creative strategy and creative brief as a sort of litmus test. If it passes, or better yet matches completely, you will know you likely have a sensible, executable, and (hopefully) effective premise for an ad. If this comparison brings about questions or conflicting information between your strategy and your existing idea, you may need to rethink the content or message.

NOW FOR THE GOOD NEWS . . .

Most people, especially those in business for themselves, intrinsically enjoy being creative. As an entrepreneur, it is likely that you do too. (Of course, if you dread the creative process, or feel you do not have a creative bone in your body, that perfectly fine, too. This chapter will give you a few outsourcing solutions to help get the job done.)

We have finally come to that point where you get to spread your artistic wings and get the creative juices flowing. So . . . how should you begin? First, let us walk through a process of outlining details relevant to your business that will help to shape the creative message. This process, better known as a *creative brief,* is common among advertising agencies. While it may take on different shapes and forms, some more elaborate or in-depth than others, the basis for all creative briefs is the same: it is an outline of important factors that will aid you in drawing a conclusion about the single most important message you can get across to your potential customer, better know as the *single basic benefit.* The single basic benefit is the most important piece of the puzzle when working through your creative brief.

THE CREATIVE BRIEF

The creative brief, in its simplest terms, is an outline (and reiteration, in some cases) of the following: your objectives, target market and key influencers, competitors, product/service features, single basic benefit, supporting benefits, tone of the advertising, current audience perception and behavior, desired audience perception and behavior, desired action, and, lastly, necessary musts. Let's look at each of these individually, along with some descriptions and examples:

Objectives

What do you hope to accomplish with the ad? Your *objectives* can be stated as they relate to your creative message, your media, or both. State the effect you hope your advertising will have on your audience, but also include the timeframe, geography, or other parameters within which you hope it will happen.

> Example: To increase knowledge and awareness of our services to the point that over 50 percent of the target market selects our company as their primary supplier within six months.

Target Market and Key Influences

List and profile by demographics, geography, and psychographics the audience for your ad or campaign. You have worked through this exercise before, in both the marketing plan (in chapter 4) and in your media plan (as outlined in chapter 5). Now it is time to expand on what you know about your target market. What characteristics about your audience will help to influence your advertising message, and what do you know about the audience that we can tap into creatively?

Example: Young women, ages 18 to 22, attending colleges or universities on the east coast, who are predisposed to eating healthy, yet have difficulty maintaining that lifestyle due to the nature of college dorm life and the offerings of the school cafeteria and local eateries.

Competitors

In this brief, you should list who your competitors are—information that is also a reiteration from your marketing plan—paying special attention to where and when your competitors are appearing with their own ads and any notes you can make on what their messages are. This step of the creative brief often prompts a quick bit of research to gather recent competitors' ads, which can be a valuable reference, from a positioning standpoint. This is especially important if your advertising takes on a preemptive approach or if you need to ensure that you are putting forth a unique selling proposition with your advertising.

Example: Company X and Company Y, who service the same greater metropolis area, are both heavily running outdoor campaigns with directional messages (touting convenience) and, often, a sales promotion or special discount.

Product/Service Features

If you have a number of products or product lines, choose which one you will be focusing on in this ad or campaign and then list all of the features of your product (or service) that you may want to talk about. Be aware that, however, you will not be able to mention every feature in your advertising, so it is a good idea to prioritize them in order of relevance to the target market you have identified above.

> Example: Our toasted subs are made to order with high-quality deli meats, freshly baked rolls, and local farmers' vegetables and cheeses. The average price is below the price of our competitors. We offer extensive delivery service and extended weekend hours.

Single Basic Benefit

In order for your advertising to be as effective as possible, it should focus on one ultimate benefit to your audience, a benefit that is more needs-driven than any other benefit of your product. You should be able to state your single basic benefit in one sentence and without using any combination of multiple benefits (see example).

If you are providing a solution that none of your competition can provide, then you have a niche product and your single basic benefit may be quite obvious because it clearly differentiates you from everyone else. You will know you are putting your best foot forward because you are the only one with that message. However, in a highly competitive market, or if your product happens to be more commonplace, determining your single basic benefit may be more difficult. In this situation, you still need to decide what makes your company a better choice than any other. Perhaps it is a lesser-known benefit of your product, or perhaps it is added value that comes along with a purchase from you versus one from one of your competitors. Think of your product as superior and, in one sentence, write down why is it so.

If you are still having difficulty with this part of the brief, it is understandable. It is also normal to have some degree of apprehension when asked to sum up your business or product in one sentence, putting all of your eggs in one *benefit* basket. We recommend moving on to the next step, supporting benefits, where you will list all the benefits of your product; once those are before you, you can prioritize them based on the needs of your audience.

> Examples: (a) Our widget offers unparalleled flexibility across the broadest range of uses (a technology-driven benefit).
>
> (b) Our healthcare facility provides peace of mind to its patients (an emotionally-driven benefit).

Supporting Benefits

What attributes of your product or service are fulfilling (or will fulfill) a need for your potential customer? This brief is the place to list all of your product or service's benefits and expand on them wherever possible. As mentioned under the single basic benefit, you may want to take this step first, listing all benefits and then prioritizing them in order of importance. This will help you to determine which is the single most important benefit for you to talk about up-front in your advertising. It is also important to note that the remaining benefits (which are not your single basic benefit) also have a place in your advertising. Because they are supporting benefits, they will help to build your case and strengthen your message in the body's copy, subheads, and bulleted lists. Always think of benefits from your customers' standpoint and what needs of theirs you are fulfilling.

> Examples: (a) Our widget is more compact than similar widgets in the market; it is available in a variety of colors and metallic finishes, and can be submerged in water up to 50 feet, and comes with a back-up battery and AC adapter and can be purchased in a multi-pack at a discounted price per unit.
>
> (b) Our healthcare facility has a nationally ranked emergency room with express service for minor injuries. Our nurses have been rated as the friendliest in the region. Test results are available online through a secure, pass-coded page. Our newly built parking deck has a covered walkway leading directly into our main lobby and registration area.

Tone of the Advertising

Think about the reputation you would like for your company and its products. What is the attitude of your business? When you think about the tone of your advertising, think about the emotions that you want to conjure up in your readers and listeners, along with the impression that you hope they are left with. For instance, if you may want to be viewed as quirky, yet knowledgeable and easy to approach. This tone may best serve an investment company targeting recent college graduates, and yet may not be sophisticated or serious enough for older generations. In this case, a sincere and professional attitude may serve you better. This is just one example of how a similar business could take on different attitudes, or advertising tones, depending on the market with which they are communicating. You may also select your tone based on the image you are hoping to build for your business to set yourself apart from your competitors. In this way, your advertising tone takes on many similarities to your branding, as discussed in chapter 3.

> Examples: (a) The tone of the ad is honest and believable, sincere and friendly. (A good tone to put forward for a law firm, perhaps, that is hoping to attract clients by positioning itself as trustworthy and approachable.)
>
> (b) The tone of the ad is hard-hitting, a bit frightening, and makes one feel a little guilty. (A likely approach for advertising products that we know we should purchase, but have put off, such as life insurance.)

Note that in example A, the tone reflects the attitudes which the company, in this case a law firm, wishes to project, but in example B, the tone of the advertising plays off of the emotional triggers of the audience, rather than connecting the company with these emotions. In turn, the company and its product (life insurance) would be positioned as a solution.

Current Audience Perception and Behavior

If your business has an existing customer base and/or you have run some advertising already, what do your customers and potential customers think and feel about you and your products? What behaviors are typical of your customers when interacting with your product? Are these tendencies positive or negative? If you do not know the answers to these questions, you should consider asking them of your customers when you are with them. Of course, time may not allow for such one-on-one interaction, nor are you guaranteed that your customers would be completely honest with you. A good alternative might be to place a feedback box in your store or office where customers can anonymously leave comments and answer your questions at their leisure. You might also consider mailing or e-mailing customers a survey, thereby gaining information about them while also showing your customers that you care about their opinions.

Being that you are an entrepreneur, however, means that you are likely working with a new start-up business, and this type of customer feedback may not yet exist. This makes the next step, stating your desired audience perception and behavior, all that much more important, so that you may create a baseline of what you hope to accomplish with your advertising and have a something to check your effectiveness against. Be sure to revisit your statement of desire once you do have this feedback from your customers to ensure that you are still on target with your goals.

Example: My customer base perceives my hot dog shop as a quick meal alternative, with unique ingredients and a hometown feel. They are willing to travel a great distance for the experience.

Desired Audience Perception and Behavior

In contrast to your *current* audience perceptions and behaviors, your *desired* audience perceptions and behaviors is where you get to dream a little. You should not approach these dreams in a weird, dancing elephants sort of way, but rather, as your vision of the perfect customer. You need to define, ideally, what you want your customers to think of you, your business, and your product(s). If things are running smoothly and business is good, your desires may not be that different than your customers' current perceptions and behaviors. Remember, there is always room for improvement, and if you are just starting out, you will want to set your goals of what you hope your customers' perceptions and behaviors will eventually be, as we stated earlier.

One way to uncover your desired audience's perceptions and behaviors is to examine those of your ideal existing customer. Perhaps there is one person who fits the bill more than anyone else. What sets them apart (aside from purchases, of course)? Something drives them to be your most loyal champion. In a way, their perception of your business sets a bar for all of your customers, not unlike your own perceptions of your business, which is also a good place to start.

Another good question to ask yourself is, "What perception of my company/product and customer behavior will make my business a success?"

> Example: We want our steakhouse to be viewed as a comfortable family dining experience, easily accessible from the main highway, with an affordable menu selection.

Desired Action

What is it, really, that you would like your readers and listeners of your advertising to do? Is it picking up the phone and place an order? Is it stopping by your location? This may be the simplest statement you will have to develop in this creative brief. What audience action will affect your bottom line the most? After all, you are investing in advertising to get a return on your investment, right?

Your *desired action* should manifest itself in your creative execution as a function for making contact by the reader or listener. It could come simply in the form of a web address, or a more elaborate, and immediate form of *call to action,* such as an order form. However, the idea of having a call to action in one's ads is often something that eludes many advertisers. Have you ever seen an ad and thought, "Man, that's really clever and I could really use one of those (products)," only to realize that nowhere on the ad was there a place to contact the company or telling where you could find more information about where to buy the product? Unless you are so well-known that everyone seeing your ads knows where to find your product (like McDonald's), or you are strictly running a branding ad and your hope is for your business to become "top-of-mind" for when a need does arise, you cannot afford to leave out this type of information and you are committing a critical error in creative execution if you do.

> Desired Action Example: I want readers to place an order for tickets.
> Call to Action Example: To order tickets for this weekend's performance, call 1-888-CHEAPTIX, or check us out online at www.supercheaptickets. com/opera

Necessary Musts

To ensure that the people involved with creating and executing your advertising have all of the proper and necessary information, list the details of your company that should be considered in your ad, such as the company's proper name, logo(s), phone numbers, web address, mailing address (or at least a street address and city), simple directional maps, copyrights and trademarks, as well as any other identifiers you may use, such as slogans or taglines. These elements, and how they are presented, are especially important as you develop a consistent look for your advertising. While not all of the elements may be used every time (for instance, due to the space limitations and read-time of billboards, street addresses and phone numbers are often left off), everything should be listed here so that it may at least be considered.

> Example: Jonathan Nimble's Big Store of Thimbles
> 123 Sewing Paradise Lane
> Beverly Hills, CA 90210
> www.jnbst.net   888.THIMBLE.ME

DO YOU HAVE A UNIQUE SELLING PROPOSITION (USP)?

Once your creative brief is complete, you will know the following:

- Who you are talking to, and what they already think about your company or product (if anything)
- What the competition looks like within your market and how they are speaking to your potential customers
- What features and benefits you hope to convey in your advertising, along with the single most important (basic) benefit that your advertising needs to focus on
- What you hope to accomplish with the advertising.

It is the answers to these answers that will now come together to help form your *creative approach*. For instance, if you are able to determine from the creative brief that you do, in fact, have a distinct competitive advantage, your best creative approach option is a *unique selling proposition (USP)*, whereby your advertising focuses on this differentiating factor. This is just one creative approach, but there are others.

OTHER CREATIVE APPROACHES

Donald E. Parente, in *Advertising Campaign Strategy: A Guide To Marketing Communications Plans*, indicated that, in addition to the *unique selling proposition*, there are six additional approaches that an advertisement or campaign can take:

Generic Strategy—A straightforward claim about the product or benefit, without positioning or statement of superiority.

Preemptive Claim—An attempt to convince the consumer that your product is superior, upstaging the competition by being the first to lay claim to a key benefit.

Brand Image Strategy—An attempt to build, reinforce, or change the consumer's attitude towards your brand, concentrates on psychological or emotional appeal.

Product Positioning—Differentiating your product or brand from the competition by making a strong and continuous statement about the benefits of your product in relationship to your competitors. This approach is useful in attempts to gain market share.

Resonance Approach—Attempts to bring to mind stored experiences of potential customers in order to give your product a relevant context within their lives. This is easier to accomplish when your brand has a history of emotional connection to its customers, but is also appropriate when your product has few differentiating characteristics.

Affective Strategy—Attempts to form a strong emotional connection between the brand and the consumer, without a strong selling emphasis.

As Parente is quick to point out, these seven approaches do not have to work on an individual basis, often overlap, and may be used in combination with another approach. For instance, you may employ a brand image approach in conjunction with a resonance approach. Think about each one of these approaches as you analyze your creative brief and your points of differentiation to decide which is the most appropriate for your advertising.

IMPORTANT ASPECTS OF AN AD

Often in marketing and advertising, you will hear creative people talking about the "big idea," and it would appear that much of their resources and energy are devoted to developing, or better yet, stumbling upon that big idea. Who could blame them? It is often the big idea that gets noticed and talked about the most. For some companies, it is the reason why they are the leader in their industry. The big idea could be a tagline, a logo, a character, or even a personality. Below are some examples of big ideas that have withstood the test of time and, in the process, created a marketing legend. See if you can recognize a few of these:

- A bunny that keeps going, and going, and going
- Provides great taste and is less filling
- A repair man who never has work because the appliances are so reliable
- Cookies so good that they had to be made by elves
- Even though it is fast food, you can still have it your way
- A fleet of brown-uniformed delivery people, working for you

Notice that these have been stated not using their more recognizable taglines or slogans, but rather as the premise for the advertising. Each premise has become a common and consistent thread throughout many years of advertising and across multiple campaigns, and each time it is used it reinforces the message, builds the brand, and creates stronger recognition with the audience. In turn, this results in a comfort level within your target market and increases the likelihood that your customer will become loyal to your products and your company.

With all of this in mind, it is not imperative that you come up with a big idea in your advertising. What is important is that you pay close attention to the development of your message and your advertising to make sure that it is *memorable, relevant, unique,* and *informative*.

What makes advertising *memorable*? You want your advertising to leave an impression with your audience. Maybe you have made a statement that is thought provoking, or an observation about something that the consumer would not have normally made. It could be memorable because of a dramatic image or a funny tune that people cannot get out of their heads.

One approach for creating a memorable ad that is considered effective by many advertising professionals is to *disrupt expectations*. Catch people off guard with something unexpected. This can be done with a play on words, such as a headline in a sporting goods store's ad that reads "Somewhere Over the Crossbow." While a lifetime of experiences tells us to expect the word "rainbow," replacing the word with something as off-the-wall as the word "crossbow" may be enough to stop the reader, get them to engage the visual, and read further into the ad.

This form of disruption can also be achieved through visuals, and given the advances in special effects, graphic design software, and photo retouching, the possibilities are endless. Take, for instance, a well-known and disruptive visual of a cow protesting the consumption of burgers, and asking people to "EAT MOR CHIKIN." By placing this spokesperson outside of its mall franchises in the form of a life-size cutout, a famous fast-food chicken restaurant delivers the unexpected and then provides a solution for anyone who buys in to the cow's philosophy.

It is also important to be relevant. While some of the pressure is put on your media placement to be in the right place at the right time and in front of the right audience, this is also a function of the creative. Are you properly conveying that you offer *solutions* to your consumers' *needs*? Are you hitting them at their peak time to make a purchase? For instance, digital outdoor displays now allow for a changing message versus the static paper or vinyl billboard. If you are a fast food chain, you can now advertise breakfast in the morning, regular menu items the rest of the day, and change it over in the late evening to remind drivers that your drive-thru window is open until 2 A.M. In this case, the medium has not changed, but rather the message has.

Be unique! There is no better way to say it. Put your best, most differentiating foot forward. Are you offering something that no one else offers? If so, tout it. If not, find a way to be different. Look at what your competitors are doing creatively. If you are advertising within the same media, create an ad that is different. Talk to your media sales representative about unique opportunities within their publication or on their station, and then craft a message around that opportunity that makes sense. It is often worth the investment to put an ad out that is not the norm, simply because it cuts through the clutter. For instance, if you are operating a brewpub and advertising in a local lifestyle publication, place your ad outside of the typical restaurant listings pages, and ask the publication if you can tip-on, or glue on, one of your custom coasters to your ad. Why? Stopping power. There is something tactile about putting a coaster in someone's hand, and it is even better if the coaster can be returned to the brewpub for a discount or special offer.

Finally, be informative. Notice that we did not say overly informative. Many advertisers attempt to put to much information into an ad that they eave the reader or listener with no desire to engage the ad or take further action. Provide enough information so that the consumer is clear on what you are advertising and is clear on what they need to do as a next step. Intentionally leaving some information out is fine, if you hope to tease your audience or entice them to follow through to learn more, but be sure to not be confusing or overly vague.

ELEMENTS OF AN AD

While there is no set formula for what must be included in your advertising, there are typical elements that go into most ads. First we will focus on the elements of print advertising, as they are the easiest to understand and are most likely where your creative development will begin. These elements include the headline, subhead, body copy, visual, and sign-off. Let's examine these one by one.

The *headline* of your ad is often the first point of contact with a reader and conveys your primary message to the audience. Often a bold or intriguing statement, there is a lot of pressure put on your headline because it not only gives your first impression, it is the basis upon which the reader will make his decision about whether or not the ad is for him and if he engage the ad any further. A headline will very often have some connection to your single basic benefit, as discussed in the creative brief earlier. It may lay it all on the line and simply state the benefit, or it may tease the reader or allude to the benefit in some way. A headline can ask a question, such as "Are you feelin' like steak tonight?" in which case the headline sets up a problem and, hopefully, the rest of the ad provides a solution. A headline can be one word or an entire sentence. While it is important to be grammatically correct throughout your advertising, sentence fragments or other techniques are often used to get attention, especially when the visual completes the thought. For instance, a travel service running an ad that shows a couple relaxing on a tropical island may run a headline that reads "When you really, really need to get away."

The *subhead*, typically found below the headline, builds on the ad's first impression. Visually, the subhead often takes a backseat to the headline in font size, shape, and/or being noticed, however, it can be just as important as the headline. Subheads very often provide supporting benefits to the headline and begin to provide a solution (if the headline presents a "problem") while also helping the reader to connect with the ad further and find reason to engage the body copy.

The *body copy* of the ad is just what it sounds like . . . the bulk of the information that you wish to provide. Often presented in paragraph form, or at least as bulleted information, the body copy should provide everything your reader needs to know about your product or service in order for her to make an educated decision about what you have to offer. If you intentionally choose to leave information out, you should, at the minimum, provide a means of contact for her to get in touch with you or your business, or a web address where she can get the information on her own. Vagueness is acceptable in advertising, as long as you can and do provide the information or way to get the information at some point without being misleading. Most importantly, be sure to include a call to action.

The *visual* of an ad can take on many forms. The most common forms of visuals in advertisements are photographs or illustrations, but there are times when a visual is simply the headline or the company's logo. The visual, like the headline and subhead of the ad, helps to draw the reader into the ad. The visual is likely to trigger the quickest emotional response out of all the elements in the ad, and will make the reader feel a certain way about your product or company. For this reason, it is important to pay attention to the quality of the visual (and the entire ad, for that matter), as your target market will associate its quality with the quality of your products and services. These days, readers react poorly to digital photography that is blurry or low-resolution, because it looks and feels cheap, unimportant, and rushed. These are the attributes you would like to have associated with your business.

The visual also plays another important role in your advertising: the role of connecting with the target market because they see themselves, figuratively, in the ads. When selecting photography or illustrations to use in your advertising, be sure to pay attention to the demographics of your target market. When it is appropriate to show people in your ad, try to use people who are similar in age, gender, income level, and so on to those whom you are trying to attract. If you are showing a setting, pay attention to the geography of the photo, such as backgrounds and building styles. When your readers can see themselves in your ad, they can assume that the product is meant for them.

Finally, the *sign-off* should include the necessary musts, also outlined in the creative brief, that should be present in the ad to ensure that the reader knows whose ad it is, where and how he may contact you, or what next steps are available to him. The sign-off should include your logo, if it is not otherwise present in the ad as part of the visual, along with your contact information. Relevant information that was not included in the body copy should also be part of the sign-off, such as store hours and directions or a map. For some ads, it is necessary to include some form of due diligence, or statement of responsibility. For instance, ads for casinos or other forms of gambling often include a Web site or phone number for anyone who may have a gambling problem.

This, like small type and disclaimers, often falls at the bottom of an ad and/or serves as part of the sign-off.

When it comes to other forms of advertising, such as radio and television spots, you will need to look at the elements in a slightly different fashion while remembering what you used to accomplish your print advertising and why it was there. While the approach and terminology may differ, the information included is much the same. Television, like print but unlike radio, has a visual to engage the viewer, it just happens to feature action rather than a still image. Television should present an opportunity that you do not have in print, since you can take the visual to the next level and now show your target market interacting with your product or better expressing emotion. The actors or subjects in your television commercial can convey their own thoughts through speaking roles rather than forcing a reader to engage the body copy.

Radio, on the other hand, relies completely on the sense of sound and a well-written script. Like television, it allows a listener to engage the ad without making them read body copy, but now, unlike print and television, the visual is completely up to the listener. In one way, it forces the sounds and descriptions to be a lot more vivid to ensure that the right visual is conveyed. However, allowing the listener to create her own visual is a nice way to ensure that she sees herself in the ad. In a way, it forces the listener to create the ideal scenario of interaction with your product or business . . . if your script includes all of the necessary information. In this way, the script for radio does the job of the body copy, visual, and the sign-off. Headlines and subheads, when carried over from print ads in the same campaign, are often used at some point in a radio script or as a visual or spoken part of a television spot to ensure consistency and continuity with the other advertisements.

BEING CREATIVE

Hopefully by now you feel that you have the proper tools to begin crafting your message and thinking about the visuals of your advertising. What we wish we could do is help you to be creative (or more creative). Unfortunately, creativity is personal and subjective. The good news is that everyone has some degree of creativity, and the more people you involve, the more likely you are to develop creatively strong and effective advertising. Some people obviously have more creativity than others, and if you can identify these people within your company, whether they are in a marketing role or not, gather them together and present them with the challenge. Ask them to review the outline of information you have now created, your creative brief, and ask them to brainstorm to develop what they would envision as effective advertising. If these people are not available to you within your own company, get a group of friends or business associates together. It is likely that your employees or friends will appreciate and enjoy the opportunity to play a role in the creation of materials that will be seen publicly, and if you reward them for contributing or helping to shape what ends up being your actual ad . . . even better. You never know where a big idea will come from, and when you are brainstorming, remember, there are no bad ideas.

Another important step in developing strong creative and effective advertising is getting early feedback. Whether you have a group of individuals brainstorming for you, or you are taking on the creative process yourself, always present your ideas to people outside of the project. Family and friends always make great informal focus groups, and while you may have to set up the scenario a little if they are not familiar with your entrepreneurial business or product, you should at least be able to get a sense for whether or not your message is easily conveyed and understandable. If you are lucky enough to show the thinking to someone who is also part of your target market, you may even learn if the ad conjures up the right emotional response and might drive someone to take action.

OUTSIDE ASSISTANCE

We know that sometimes, for any of a number of reasons, it makes more sense to put the task of creating advertising into the hands of someone else. Given all of the work involved with building an entrepreneurial business from the ground up, you may not have the time to devote to creating ads, even if you have the capability and desire to do so. Luckily, there are a number of resources you can turn to for this type of assistance. You could hire a graphic designer or freelance designer/artist. Just be sure that the person has prior experience designing advertising. Depending on the level of their expertise, you may find that she is more than capable of some work, like page layout and design, photography, illustration work, and so on, but is lacking in other areas, such as writing copy. The more of these capabilities this individual possesses, the less work you will have to do in guiding her.

A better option, if budget permits, is to hire an advertising agency. Unlike a freelance graphic designer with possible limitations and resources, an agency should provide everything you need in the way of capabilities. From conceptual thinking and copywriting to art direction, design and file preparation, an agency is a one-stop shop for your advertising needs. Most agencies also take or direct their own photography and have the required resources for audio and video production. Just be sure the agency is up-front with you about costs and that you are up-front with them about your expectations. There should be no surprises, and everyone involved should understand his role. This holds true when working with a freelancer as well. Be sure to ask for estimated costs up-front, and discuss what the agency may able to bring to the table in the way of other capabilities of which you might want to take advantage at some point, such as media planning and placement.

The stronger you can make your relationship with an advertising agency, the better off you will be. Share as much information with them as possible, including the creative brief if you have written one. They, too, will work through a similar process of collecting information, especially if someone in your company has not previously done so. The details of this process should be discussed and agreed upon before any conceptual thinking begins. The benefits to using an agency are numerous, but one of the most important is the fact that they provide an outside perspective. They are not you, and they can more easily put themselves into the shoes of your target market. Other benefits include their creative ability, and the fact that they have already pulled together a creative team to do this type of work. This is what they do . . . they create *memorable, relevant, unique,* and *informative* advertising. Good agencies also have a deep understanding of design, such as effective and appealing layouts and fonts, the psychology of color, and design trends across various industries. Agencies also bring with them an arsenal of contacts and relationships with other service providers, such as photographers, sign companies, and printers, and knowledge of print specifications and file preparation for all forms of media.

In some markets, there may be additional outsourcing opportunities that include local advertising and marketing clubs and college marketing classes and graphic design classes. Depending on your type of business, the amount of time you can allow for the development of ideas, and their willingness and capability to help out, you might be able to present these groups or classes with the challenge of creating your advertising, and they may take it on as a project or assignment. The downside is that you are not guaranteed to get results this way, nor is there a strong understanding of the real world (in the case of the college classes). While the ideas may be clever or interesting, you run a higher degree of risk that they are simply not applicable. The upside, however, is that these projects may not cost you anything. Just be wary . . . you get what you pay for.

RECAP

Having spent a good deal of time focusing on just the creative portion of your advertising, you can now see the importance of your overall advertising message. Chapter 7 focused on the first creative portion of your advertising plan, the development and crafting of your message. In particular, this chapter is designed to help you create your overall creative brief. The creative brief provides an outline and direction for the development of all other advertising creative components. Because of this, the creative brief must be developed with careful thought.

The chapter concluded by examining what elements need to go into an ad, and offers many suggestions for the development of a strategy in executing your message. This chapter examined the following important areas:

- Where creativity fits into the plan
- How to take advantage of creativity by crafting your message
- Hints about which elements of the advertisement are important, and a discussion of those elements
- Thoughts about getting outside assistance and the development of a strategy.

Chapter 8 will take the advertising and media plans and marry them with additional IMC variables. It also introduces readers to the integrated marketing communication mix (the IMC mix) and offers suggestions regarding the exploitation of these additional communications tools.

SUMMARY

- ☑ If you have a great idea for an ad, and it fits with the elements you have outlined in your creative brief, do not be afraid to run with it.
- ☑ Share your creative brief with everyone involved in the creative process and crafting your message, especially your advertising agency.
- ☑ Continuity in your messages is key.
- ☑ Make sure your advertising is memorable, relevant, unique, and informative.
- ☑ Do not forget to include a call to action!

8

Integrating Other Marketing Communications Components into Your Executions

At the end of chapter 1, as we outlined the template of your marketing plan, we asked the question, "What line of attack are you developing for your marketing mix?," and when it came to possible communications tactics, we mentioned the following: advertising, branding, cybermarketing, direct marketing, personal selling, public relations/publicity, and sales promotions. These tactics, or Integrated Marketing Communications (IMC) variables, were defined briefly in chapter 6 as they relate to other components in your advertising plan. This chapter expands on their description and how they interact with the advertising and media plan you have just created. Since we have already discussed the development and placement of your advertising at length, and chapter 3 was entirely about branding, it is now appropriate to focus on the last five variables: cybermarketing, direct marketing, personal selling, public relations/publicity, and sales promotions.

CYBERMARKETING

Any advertising or communications done utilizing the Internet, databases or other forms of computer technology delivery are referred to as *cybermarketing*. Online ads, computer game placements, DVDs, videos, database marketing and customer relationship marketing, as well as other types of advertising, are used as tactical executions within this area. We have already discussed online advertising to some degree, because it has become so prevalent in many advertisers' plans, and, as we have stated before, is mow considered a traditional form of advertising by some. For the sake of argument, however, we will include it in this discussion about cybermarketing, since it is very relevant.

The reason cybermarketing has become so widely used is two-fold: it allows marketing communications to be both *personalized* and *interactive.*

Cybermarketing also more affordably allows messages to be delivered in ways that had previously been expensive. Consider the cost of printing a large product catalog and then mailing it to potential customers. Today, a PDF version of that same information can be downloaded from your Web site or sent to potential customers in an email, without ever sending it to print. This also saves valuable time and costs when changes need to occur within the catalog, an event that would, in the days of more traditional publishing, create the need for a reprint.

The following are more examples of cybermarketing. As they are mentioned, consider what had been necessary prior to the use of e-mail, the Internet, and high-capacity CDs, DVDs, and USB drives.

- E-mail marketing and e-newsletters
- CD-ROM and DVD information kits, presentations, product catalogs/ sales literature, and so on
- Electronic Data Interchange (EDI)—the electronic exchange of business documents across a network with vendors or customers
- Maintaining a presence on account with online social networking sites, such as Facebook, MySpace, Twitter, Digg, Plaxo, Flickr, YouTube, and many more
- Creation of a product, company or industry blog
- Search engine optimization.

There was a time when just having a Web site meant that you were in the cybermarketing game, but this is not so anymore. Now, you must be part of the interaction, either by inserting yourself into the existing flow of social network interaction, or by creating your own means for interacting with your customers. Just remember, the online world never shuts down. It is highly interactive, personalized, and nonstop. The fact that your customers can now gather information instantly, 24 hours per day, 365 days per year, means that your response time needs to be just as instant. Do not let your Web site grow stagnant, and make sure that someone in your company is checking emails and responding to them daily, if possible. Your cybermarketing efforts can lend a lot of credibility to your company if you can keep the lines of communications open and flowing, but allowing the communication to break down could cause you to lose customers very quickly.

According to the U.S. Department of Consumer Affairs, it costs five times more to gain a new customer than to retain an existing one. The reality today is that, because of the vast amount of information online, the ease of someone conducting his own research, and the general decrease in brand loyalty, the challenge of *retention* has never been greater. That said, thanks to cybermarketing and advances in technology, the opportunity to deliver great customer service through quick response and personal attention has never been easier, if you are willing to do the work.

DIRECT MARKETING

Direct marketing is any effort a company may put in place to communicate directly with customers and potential customers while also providing a mechanism for them to take action or respond in some way. This response may take on any number of forms, such as the completion of a survey, a visit to an office or store, or a phone call to make a purchase or a request for more information.

Because direct marketing creates an immediate buyer-seller connection, this form of communication, or selling, is called *relationship marketing*.

Direct marketing is used to stimulate immediate and measurable responses and sales, and therefore has a strong advantage over other forms of marketing when it comes to *accountability.*

Direct marketing can utilize any form of media, as long as the message is looking for an immediate customer action. Direct marketing usually takes on one of three forms: direct response advertising, telemarketing, or direct selling.

Direct response advertising includes the use of direct mail, print media, broadcast, or electronic media in order to deliver the mechanism for obtaining a customer's response. *Couponing* is frequently used as a direct marketing method, especially in print or as an electronically downloadable piece of marketing collateral. *Infomercials* are common forms of direct marketing on television. Think about the response mechanism of a half-hour infomercial. How often do you see the cost of the product and the toll-free number appear? While this type of marketing can be very expensive to create and execute, the return can be very high as well, and from what we have learned so far, it is immediate. Infomercials work so well that entire television channels have taken on that format, broadcasting 24 hours per day, seven days per week; among the best known are the Home Shopping Network and QVC.

Telemarketing is the use of the telephone to solicit and close sales. The automation of such telemarketing calls has added a level of convenience and cost savings (to business owners) but has eliminated a level of personal interaction. Furthermore, while the success of infomercials and home shopping networks has increased, and more people turn to the Internet and e-marketing to make purchases, a growing resistance to telemarketing has developed, so much so that the National Do Not Call Registry has been implemented to eliminate contact from telemarketers, making this approach difficult and unfavorable.

Direct selling is generally a function of a sales department and will be explained later in this chapter, under personal selling.

When cybermarketing crosses over with direct response advertising, the result is a form of direct e-marketing, or better yet e-mail marketing, that has now taken the world by storm. Sometimes this is a welcome, opted-in form of buying and selling, but all too often it is unwelcome and better known as "spam." Keep this in mind when creating a database or list of individuals or businesses to whom you will be sending your direct mail or e-mail. If the communications are wanted (the recipient has opted-in), you will nurture the relationship with every piece of direct marketing that you send them. On the other hand, if they do not want to hear from you, and you have given them no way to opt out, you will have destroyed any chance of gaining them as a customer and ruined your credibility. Remember the power of word of mouth.

DATABASE MARKETING

This brings us to a very important aspect of direct marketing: *database marketing*. Database marketing is exactly what it sounds like, building, managing, and maintaining a database of customers and potential customers through a variety of means to accomplish the most effective and relevant direct marketing possible.

Whether you are starting with an existing database of potential customers, such as a member list of your local Chamber of Commerce, or you are starting from scratch to develop a new database of prospects, the more current, accurate, and relevant information you have about these individuals, the better the database will be as a successful sales tool.

Below is a list of the basic customer information you should attempt to collect from each person or business when building your database:

- Names and full addresses (ZIP codes are crucial)
- Telephone numbers (day, night, and mobile)
- E-mail address
- Date of birth (especially if you offer "birthday rewards" or some similar feature)
- Demographic information (age, gender, marital status, education, income, occupation, hobbies, family info, etc.)
- Purchase history, amounts, frequency, and most recent activity (pending software capabilities)
- Anniversary date of first purchase
- (For business customers) North American Industrial Classification System (NAICS) code, industry, number of employees, annual revenue.

Think of your database as having three parts: the data you have gathered from existing lists, such as organizations to which you belong, the data you add from list rentals through an outside source, and the data you continuously add regarding every new customer. You may even have an operational system in place that handles sales, inventory, or other business functions. The trick, if not already in place, is to make sure that the customer information you collect makes it into your marketing database. Although it may depend on the software capabilities of your sales system, attempt to add as much relevant information about the buying habits of your existing customers as possible. For instance, if you own a lawn and garden center, you may keep a record of customers who have recently made multiple purchases of patio and outdoor furniture, landscaping services, or other large-ticket items. Because of their predisposition to buy and loyalty to your store, this list of customers could be isolated during the pre-holiday season to send them a special offer and quite possibly entice them back into your store during a time when they are not normally considering your venue as a shopping option.

Another good data collection practice when communicating with your existing customer base is to offer incentives to them for providing information about family and friends. This is a common practice online and through e-mail marketing, and many customers are often quick to offer up the e-mail addresses of 5 to 10 acquaintances if there is something in it for them.

PERSONAL SELLING

Personal selling is a face-to-face, often one-on-one, form of communication during which the seller attempts to persuade an individual to make a purchase. Personal selling is the primary function of a company's sales force, and while it is usually thought of more often in a business-to-business scenario, the use of personal selling is also quite common and effective in business-to-consumer situations. In fact, with telemarketing becoming more difficult, personal selling has enjoyed a resurgence in recent years. Businesses ranging from financial planner to custom window fabricators have all found a way to get face-to-face time with prospects. Popular businesses, such as Tastefully Simple and Pampered Chef, rely on an army of personal selling professionals who arrange household gatherings to make their pitch. Like the Avon and Tupperware parties of the past, this form of personal selling is convenient for the buyer, and is fun and social. The response mechanism of actual purchases is immediate as well, so, as a direct marketing technique, the advantages hold true (i.e., immediate and measurable response and sales).

Personal selling offers four distinct advantages as a marketing tool.

- *Instant feedback*—The presenter can quickly tell if the prospect fully understands the sales presentation and modify his or her pitch if necessary.
- *Product demonstrations*—This is one of the few scenarios where the potential customer can witness actual demonstration firsthand.
- *Powerful selling position*—The seller has the advantage of being in a situation that potentially could make it difficult for the buyer to say "No." Be sure to eliminate any discomfort that the customer may have, but also know that you have the customer's full attention and can address any issues or concerns.
- *Relationship building*—There is no better way to get to know someone than to sit down with them face-to-face. As the seller, this gives you an opportunity to build trust and comfort. If this is to become an ongoing buyer-seller relationship, the buyer will need to feel both.

The interesting thing about personal selling is that it is almost the complete opposite of advertising using traditional mass media. Instead of positioning your message in front of hundreds of thousands of individuals, you are sitting down with one person, or a very small group of people, to deliver that message just to them. However, both are valid, effective, and widely used marketing techniques. When direct selling is integrated into the same marketing effort or campaign as mass media-based sales, you will start to see the power of a full IMC plan.

PUBLIC RELATIONS / PUBLICITY

Public Relations (PR), like advertising, uses the media to deliver a message to the general public, however, the major difference is that PR is unpaid. You do not pay for airtime on broadcast or space in print media for PR. Rather,

PR managers rely on newsworthy events and stories to garner the attention of local media. The delivery of the message then comes from the voice of the media, such as the local television news, newspaper columnist, or on-air radio personality. This can be a good thing, as the endorsement is coming from a third party, but it is important to realize that this is also uncontrollable to some degree, and sometimes PR that was meant to produce goodwill for the company can backfire and produce negative publicity.

Publicity is a subfunction of public relations. It is the effort of generating news about a company, an individual within a company, a product or service, or the company's involvement with an outside organization or an event at or involving the company or its employees. Publicity is often viewed as free, although there are inherent costs associated with it, such as the writing of the stories or articles. Regardless, even with the costs involved, which are relatively low, public relations and publicity offer a great return on investment.

As an entrepreneurial business, whether you are dealing with trade or consumer PR, the objectives of your PR efforts will tend to fall into one of the following categories:

- *Reputation management*—This involves creating and managing the reputation of the company, hopefully for the best, but sometimes the effort can also be damage control following a problem or negative situation.
- *Public affairs management*—Managing communications to elected officials or regulatory bodies, especially when the actions of the company contribute to the public good in some way.
- *Special events management*—Managing, from a PR standpoint, the efforts surrounding a sporting event, sponsorship of a cultural event, or some other community-oriented event, thus ensuring the integration of other IMC variables.
- *Speech writing*—Speech writing can be done for various organizational personnel within your company or to provide them with talking points, possible written answers to questions that may be asked of company officials (such as during a press conference). Consistency in messages is critical between all PR efforts and other marketing and advertising communications.
- *Publication development*—This involves annual reports, manuals, newsletters, and other brochures. Again, consistency is key, and in this case, depending on where the literature is picked up, PR may have to carry creative elements over from advertising and other marketing pieces.

Some quick pointers to keep in mind when executing your PR efforts as part of your IMC plan are:

- Put a news or press release on paper containing all pertinent details. While the media is likely to follow up on any worthy story, do not expect reporters to do any further research. Instead, give them everything they need.
- Provide photos with captions whenever possible.

- When you have multiple pieces to get to the media, such as a release, photo(s), fact sheet, CDs, DVDs, product samples, or the like, bundle them together in a media or press kit.
- Use a professional writer when you have been offered or are going after a feature article, which are typically lengthier than most press releases.
- Offer unique experiences that people will want to talk about, such as a guided factory tour, open house, or an exhibit of your company/products somewhere publicly, such as at a local mall. The displays can be temporary, and the tours can be offered to a select group of people, such as local dignitaries, VIPs, and media representatives.

The most important thing to remember in executing your PR efforts is that this is still a means of communicating with your potential customer. While the customer may not hear the message as coming directly from you, but rather they will be exposed to it from a third party, it will still help them to formulate an opinion of your company or product and should not be taken lightly.

SALES PROMOTION

Over the past 25 years, marketing professionals have found a significantly increased value in strategic sales promotion efforts, provided that they are integrated with other IMC components. The flip side is that the increased budget allocation to sales promotion has often been at the expense of the advertising and media budget. This is due, in part, to the more personalized touch and interactivity of a promotion that consumers have come to appreciate and even seek out. As consumers, we have been conditioned to think that, if it is not on sale or does not come with some type of premium or incentive, then we are paying too much. This is not necessarily the case, but then again, perception is everything. Sales promotions, for this reason, are activities put in place to stimulate sales. A *sales promotion* offers a buyer an incentive to make a purchase through the use of either a cost savings or a value-added offer or premium. This often occurs at the point of sale, or point of purchase, but may also appear elsewhere.

There are two main types of sales promotions: the *consumer-focused promotion,* whereby the sales promotion is directed at the end-user of the product, and the *trade-focused promotion,* whereby the promotional tools are directed at someone along the chain of distribution, such as a retailer or wholesaler, in order to entice them to start carrying a product, make a larger purchase, or give preferential treatment to the supplier. We will begin by explaining trade promotions first, so that we can then focus on consumer promotions.

TRADE PROMOTIONS

Because trade promotions are directed at people within the supply chain, such as retailers and wholesalers, these incentives are, most often, a way for them to decrease their outlay of cash for your product. They can also be in the form of materials to help their promotional efforts and improve their ability to sell your product. One of the most common trade promotions is *trade allowances*. Trade allowances are the discounted amounts offered to the reseller in your supply chain in order to afford them the luxury of reducing the price on the product and making it more affordable for their particular customers. Note that not all of the trade allowance is passed along to the consumer, but rather a portion of it is often pocketed by the reseller. Trade allowances take on many different forms such as the following:

- *Off-invoice allowances*—These are deals that allow a retailer or wholesaler to deduct a fixed amount from the invoice.
- *Bill-back allowances*—These occur when the manufacturer pays a retailer for featuring the manufacturer's brand of for providing special display opportunities.
- *Slotted allowances*—These are fees paid by the manufacturer to the retailer for carrying their product; the fees are typically based on specific store shelf space, or *slots*. This allowance is a guarantee to be carried and positioned on the shelves in some fashion. This is a popular practice with grocery stores.
- *Exit fees*—This refers to a charge to a supplier for the removal of products at the end of a contracted period, which usually stipulates an average volume of consumer traffic during that timeframe.
- *Forward buying and diverting*—This is a price reduction given to a retailer or wholesaler when a large purchase is made up-front, to be stockpiled or stored, and sold over time.
- *Everyday low price (EDLP)*—A term used when a manufacturer ensures that he sells that same product for the same price at all times.
- *Efficient consumer response (ECR)*—This refers to reducing the overall costs to the retailer by developing more efficient ordering procedures and maintenance of excessive inventories.
- *Pay-for-performance*—This strategy is used when a manufacturer sets a goal with a retailer and the retailer is rewarded for meeting the sales goals or receives a trade allowance only on those products sold, as recorded by a scanning device.

In addition to the different forms of trade allowances, trade promotions can also take on the form of cooperative advertising, vendor support programs, trade contests and incentives, point-of-purchase (POP) materials such as floor decals, posters, rack danglers, ad so on, training programs, specialty advertising, and trade shows.

CONSUMER PROMOTIONS

As mentioned earlier, consumer promotions are put in place to entice the end user, or consumer, to make a purchase. While the primarily goal is to stimulate sales, there are a number of other objectives that can be accomplished during consumer promotions. These include relationship maintenance, trial stimulation, encouraging repeat use and purchases, increasing purchase frequency, new product introduction and education, new package design awareness, seasonal exploitation, and trade-ups.

Examples of consumer promotions include, but are not limited to:

- *Sampling*—This refers to delivering an actual or trial-sized product to the consumer. One popular approach to sampling is through an in-store station, common in stores such as Sam's Club.
- *Point-of-purchase couponing*—These are coupons available right where the product is picked up in the store, or where the actual purchase is made.
- *Mail- and media-delivered couponing*—Coupons mailed directly into homes, or delivered to consumers via some type of medium, such as the Sunday newspaper. Free-standing inserts (FSIs) or flyers are common examples this medium.
- *In-pack or on-pack couponing*—This approach encourages consumers to tear the coupon off the package as they check out. The coupons can either be used for the current purchase or a future purchase.
- *Premiums*—Premiums are free merchandise or other incentives, usually attained by mailing in proofs of purchase, by collecting a specific number of package proofs, or attached to the package or on a POP display to take at the time of purchase.
- *Price-off promotions*—This refers to a price reduction from the suggested retail price.
- *Bonus packs*—These are extra quantities of the product sold at the typical retail price.
- *Refunds and rebates*—These are cash discounts or reimbursements given to the consumer after they have made a purchase.
- *Contests and sweepstakes*—Consumers can win or earn cash or prizes by participating. These often apply once a purchase is made, but is not necessary in some cases (many contests and sweepstakes' rules will even note that "no purchase is necessary to win (or play)").
- *Overlay and tie-in promotions*—This refers to the execution of multiple promotional efforts at the same time, often carried out because of multiple brands involved with the same promotion. Consider the size of the promotional efforts when a new summer movie comes out and the tie-ins to fast food, grocery products, automotive, hospitality and travel products, and more.
- *Product warranties and guarantees*—This is a value-added enticement for consumers that offers a solution if something should go wrong with the product. These are sometimes presented as "limited-time" offers in order to increase their value and deliver a sense of urgency.

The key to the integration of these IMC components with your advertising and branding efforts is to always keep every effort in sight and to remember that they support each other, depend on each other, compliment each other, and, most of all, often cross paths as they run simultaneously. Your marketing communications are not independent functions, but instead, each one has an effect on the other. In order to maximize the effectiveness of your efforts, you must manage your IMC efforts as you would any other function of your business.

RECAP

Those of us involved in the development of advertising noticed, a number of years ago, that there were many elements of marketing that communicate to consumers. Additionally, we figured out that all marketing variables communicate and that all marketing variables impact not only the consumer, but each other as well. In order to get the best efficiencies for our advertising, we found that if we integrated all of the communications variables, we would have a much stronger plan that was much more efficient (more messages, less cost) than our previous efforts had been. In chapter 8, we discussed the IMC approach and focused on each of the IMC variables that can be used to generate advertising and IMC executions.

Specifically, this chapter has focused on the following:

- Cybermarketing
- The use of database marketing as part of the cybermarketing and direct marketing variables
- Direct marketing
- Personal selling
- Public relations and publicity
- Sales promotion, both trade and consumer.

The last topics we have to cover, in chapter 9, concern putting your entire plan together and measuring how well you did with your planning and executions. After implementing your executions, you will want to measure how effective the campaign was. What did you do right? What went wrong? Chapter 9 provides the answers to these questions.

SUMMARY

☑ Always think about your marketing communications with potential customers as an attempt to start a relationship.

☑ Make sure that customers and potential customers have opted in to receive your electronic mailings.

☑ Remember, every group or organization with a membership base potentially has a database of people which you may be able to tap into, with their permission of course.

☑ Publicity can be positive or negative.

☑ Consumers respond well to sales promotions when they are professionally executed and offer something of value.

9

Putting the Plan Together and Measuring Its Effectiveness

Up to this point, we have been concerned about generating enough data and information to be able to execute our advertising and integrated marketing communications (IMC) plan. This chapter concentrates on the execution of the plan and the analysis and evaluation that will follow its execution to determine how effective the plan was.

Remember, at the onset of the plan you were generating information and data that could be used in the execution. As you progressed through the chapters, you gathered enough information to create an effective and totally integrated plan. Now is the time to develop a working document that you can refer to while executing the advertising portion of your business.

Begin with a thorough review of your overall marketing plan. Make sure all elements are in place and that you have created objectives for each of the areas you want to execute. After assessing the marketing plan, revisit your advertising and IMC plan to make sure that you have not made any silly or stupid mistakes in your planning process. Re-check your objectives to make sure they are realistic, achievable, quantifiable, and time-bound. If they are not, correct them now. Your objectives will serve as your main method for evaluating the plan's effectiveness.

THE FINAL STEP

Evaluating the effectiveness of your advertising campaign is generally the final step you will take in this process. You must spend time thinking about the impact you want your advertising campaign to have on your customers and stakeholders. Because of this, we recommend that you develop your evaluative techniques *prior* to launching your advertising campaign. What, specifically, are the outcomes you are looking for? How, specifically, can they be measured? You, as the entrepreneur, must evaluate your entire plan from your mission, vision, and objectives, to your budget and tactical executions. Have you followed your plan? Why or why not? What outside environments have had an impact on the plan? How did the audiences respond to the plan? Was the response what you thought it would, or should be? How did your strategies work? Were they as effective as you thought they should be? How were the creative executions? Were your audiences happy with the creative message and voice? Did you drive sales? Did you strengthen the brand?

If you can answer "yes" to the majority of these questions, you may have an effective plan. If you answer "no," additional research is needed to find the flaws. Corrective action is often required to address faulty parts of a plan, and the sooner corrections are made, the better it is for the campaign. The remainder of this chapter offers advice in terms of evaluating and controlling for errors within your advertising campaign.

EVALUATION

The evaluation of a campaign is essential. It allows you to see the fruits of your labor and how well you developed and executed your advertising. Additionally, evaluation may provide you with additional value-added output such as:

1. *Additional productivity for the advertising campaign.* People who work in advertising are hard-working, creative individuals who sometimes get too close to their work. These professionals can become a little myopic when it comes to their own work. An outside view and evaluation may be used to point out to advertising professionals where they are on track, or when they need to make some adjustments to the work they are producing.
2. *Avoid mistakes and save time.* Mistakes in advertising are costly. Expenditures on IMC and advertising-related executions are currently in the hundreds of billions of dollars (and moving toward trillions). By planning ahead and evaluating outcomes, you can be sure that your dollar expenditures are being placed in the correct spots.
3. *The effectiveness of the overall advertising strategies and tactics can be measured.* Because these are measurable items, over time, you will begin to get a good feeling about which executions work the best. Additionally, you can track which of your media expenditures are working the best. If there are faulty strategies highlighted in the evaluation, change or delete them from the plan. If there are tactical executions that are not working at this time, delete them from the plan (or at least modify the executions).

The end of a campaign is a great time to evaluate. Often, companies and organizations do not evaluate. We cannot condone this practice, but we certainly understand why some people choose not to evaluate. Typically, entrepreneurs do not have the expertise to develop and execute an advertising evaluation. Additionally, they may not see the value in such an exercise. An evaluation program is very expensive, so at times business people may feel that they are saving money by not evaluating. (They are not; rather, the opposite is true, failing to evaluate will cost them more money spent on ineffective advertising, or, worse yet, ads that are driving customers away from their business.) Time may be another factor for explaining why entrepreneurs do not evaluate. At face value, it appears that the time needed for successful evaluations is not worth the outcome, but again, it is not true!

Some business people may not be sure specifically what to test or how to test campaigns. Finally, entrepreneurs who do not evaluate often feel that their evaluations are not objective. Whatever the case, do not fall into the trap of not evaluating. If you cannot find the time to do it, outsource the function. This is one of the most important steps you will take in your advertising development.

One question that may have occurred to you is "When should I outsource the evaluation process, and when should I do it myself?" The following section will help you to decide whether you should do it yourself or outsource. Immediately following that section is a framework for research development for the do-it-yourselfer.

HIRE IT OUT, OR DO IT YOURSELF?

One of the nice things about outsourcing tasks for your business is that you can influence your service providers to help assess the effectiveness of your advertising campaign. Almost all advertising agencies will help you to track ad placements, audience numbers, and so on. The agencies will track whether the ad was placed correctly, and note whether it actually appeared in print or was broadcast. Agencies will assist you in generating "make-goods" if something happened to your ad during its execution, for example, if the President of the United States preempts an advertisement for the State of The Union address or some other purpose. If this happens, agencies will see that the ad is run in a comparable place. In addition, agencies often help with other types of campaign evaluations, such as pre-evaluations of advertisements to ensure they are creative, believable, and effective. The paragraphs below explore many methods of evaluation and control that are often offered at part of a supplier's service, as value-added benefits, or for an additional cost (i.e., a la carte services). Please keep in mind that some types of evaluation must be created in order to assure the plan is effective. This means that, if the evaluation function is not outsourced, you must undertake the process yourself.

WHAT SHOULD WE EVALUATE?

There are, at a minimum, four distinct times during an advertising campaign when evaluations should be undertaken:

1. At the beginning of the campaign
2. At the end (a middle assessment may also be helpful) of the creative platform development
3. During the advertising campaign period when you are executing your media tactics (test concurrently with the media)
4. Post-testing (after the advertising campaign has run).

Each of these times offers the advertiser opportunities to create an evaluation and then put in controls. If your advertising campaign is not working, it needs to be changed. This section of the book examines some of the most common techniques used to evaluate advertising campaigns. There are hundreds of evaluation methods; this chapter covers the most popular and the most effective.

During the development of the advertising campaign, we recommend running a concept test. In the initial phases of the campaign, you will want to assess the value of the concept that you have created for your targeted audience. Test the concept *after* you have completed your marketing research, but *before* you develop the creative executions. The concept test will help you to get a feel for your audience's reaction to your campaign ideas. In order to undertake a concept test, first decide if you will execute the test, or if you need to outsource it. If you are using an agency, they will help you to develop the test. If you are going to do it yourself, you will need to follow the marketing research steps presented at the end of this chapter. Methods used to undertake concept testing include, but are not limited to, the following:

1. *Focus groups.* In a focus group, advertising researchers invite a small group of people in from a sample population. These 6 to 12 individuals then give their opinions about advertising executions, the product, branding, or any other item under study. Advertisers can assess the effectiveness of their message (among other uses) by undertaking focus group research.

2. *Delphi Technique.* The Delphi Technique is a specialized form of executive opinion research. The technique involves asking higher placed executives what they think about a particular advertising issue at hand. The process is secretive and all of the responses from the sample are tallied with the results shared.

3. *Scaling.* We often develop scales in research to try to figure out the strength of some body of research. Scales can be developed that explore many different areas of advertising. For example, if an advertiser wants to find out how much a consumer prefers the current brand the advertiser is featuring, advertising researchers can develop a scale to assess that strength of preference. The scale may read on one side "totally love the brand" and on the other "totally hate the brand." The results of the research are tallied and shared.

4. *In-depth personal interviews.* Because we often find that 20 percent of our customers provide us with 80 percent of our revenue, advertisers may wish to speak with their best customers in order to get their opinions on advertising issues. In-depth personal interviews allow the researcher to speak, in depth, with individuals who have positive, exciting ideas that may be beneficial to the entire advertising campaign.

5. *Questionnaires.* Questionnaires are a type of research instrument used to collect perceptions, opinions, and ideas. A series of questions are developed that speak specifically to a problem or opportunity an advertiser is experiencing. The questionnaires are sent to large sample groups whose responses will mirror what the general public is thinking (or what the population under study is thinking).

6. *Rating scales.* Rating scales ask respondents to rate individual statements based upon their personal opinions. Advertisers can then take those ratings and use them to create more effective advertising executions.

7. *Paired comparison tests.* In a paired comparison test, respondents are asked to give their opinions about a pair of like products, services, or objects. This allows advertisers to measure consumer preference based upon competing products.

8. *Projective techniques.* Projective techniques require a research respondent to project his own ideas into a story. Based upon his projections, trained researchers can make assumptions about what the respondents think.

9. *Partially structured, complete the story.* A partially completed story is developed to place a respondent in a familiar situation. Respondents are asked to complete the story while trained researchers make judgments about the respondents based upon how they complete the story.

10. *Attitude and opinion scaling.* This is a scaling technique that attempts to ask pointed, opinionated questions about an advertisement or advertising campaign. Respondents are asked to report their own attitudes and opinions regarding a particular research topic.

Please remember that concept tests have been developed to just test a concept. This is typically what is called *qualitative research,* but will give you a good idea of how well the advertising campaign's concept will be received by your audience. Qualitative research refers to acquisition of soft research that is not sampling theory-based. With qualitative research, no findings can be generalized to the overall population. In order to create numbers and generalize concepts to the general public, advertisers and researchers undertake *quantitative research.* In quantitative research, each step is important and must reflect what is occurring in the general population. Quantitative research uses a lot of sampling statistics and presents findings that can be generalized, whereas qualitative research is used to find out about opinions and ideas. It is generally used to explore concepts, and is often referred to as *exploratory research.* Although the findings cannot be generalized, they do provide advertisers and advertising researchers with a lot of important insight into concepts, advertisements, and other ideas.

After the concept test has been completed and assessed, it is a good idea to run a *copy test.* Copy testing is typically used to evaluate an individual advertisement's impact. Most major advertisements are subject to copy testing. Copy tests are used in the following settings:

- Theatre tests. These are conducted in an actual movie theatre.
- Central location tests. Test subjects are asked to report to some central location where everyone is tested in a controlled, laboratory situation.
- Television tests. These are run directly into a sample of the target market's television sets.
- Objective tests. Objective tests are given to respondents online, through the mail, or at some central location in order to gauge the sample's feelings and opinions.

Objective tests include the use of various electronic devices such as the pupilometer, the tachistoscope, the Galvanic skin response test (GSR test), and the use of various eye cameras that will track the audience's gaze and eye patterns. Copy testing is undertaken before your ads run, thus it is oftentimes referred to as "pretesting." These types of tests are best outsourced, as the person in charge of administering the tests must have a lot of training (as well as have access to the equipment needed to conduct the tests). An individual entrepreneur will probably not run enough tests to make the time and costs associated with the purchase of the required equipment worthwhile. The decision to undertake the use of these tests is totally up to each entrepreneur or advertiser, based upon information she needs for the effective execution of an advertising campaign.

After you have begun to execute your advertising campaign, you may want to undertake *concurrent testing.* Concurrent testing occurs during the execution of the campaign and allows entrepreneurs to modify or cancel the campaign's tactical executions. The two major types of concurrent testing are *tracking studies* and *coincidental studies.*

Tracking studies are a series of interviews conducted with the customer (i.e., the target audience). The studies are conducted throughout the entire campaign period. These studies will allow you to understand the effectiveness of your entire campaign and how much exposure it is creating for you. Always create your tracking schedule in advance to minimize error and to increase the validity of your research. Tracking studies will also allow you to generate data on your consumers' product satisfaction, awareness, attitudes, desires, and the amount of product usage (on average) of your market target. The most popular types of tracking studies include:

1. Dust bin checks
2. Pantry checks
3. Consumer diaries
4. Mall intercept studies
5. Scanner data (typically you will want to contact Information Resources, Inc., (commonly known as IRI) for information on how to get and use their scanner data for your product or products).

Coincidental studies are used to check for responses to the communications that you are executing. With a coincidental study, you will be able to check the amounts of exposure to your various advertising executions and your audience's reaction to that exposure for each of your advertising media vehicles. Typically, coincidental studies are undertaken for broadcast media (in particular, radio and television). In a coincidental study, members of your targeted audience are contacted during the airing of your commercial message. The objective is to find out which radio stations and television stations the audience is listening to or watching. From these data, you can ascertain if your message is being seen and/or heard. Although an effective technique, this approach may not be worth the cost for smaller-sized entrepreneurial operations due to the small amount of data and the specific nature of those data. The cost ranges for these types of tests vary widely and depend on the number of variables the entrepreneur wants to consider.

Post-testing is an essential for advertising. Although it is closely related to concurrent testing, post-testing occurs after the entire campaign has been completed, and is used to assess the impact of your campaign. Two important reasons to post-test are to generate an objective analysis of the impact of your advertising (and other IMC elements) and to develop a metric system for use in the development of future campaigns.

In post-testing, you (the researcher) want to identify the impact your entire campaign has had on your targeted audience. Additionally, you want to measure any behavioral changes that may have occurred with your audience. In order to accomplish this, you must create metrics or bases to be used for all future campaigns. The biggest drawback to post-testing is the development of effective benchmarks that will allow you to generate meaningful data. It is recommended that you utilize both concurrent and post-testing in order to get the best results. Another way to make sure you have meaningful benchmarks is to undertake a pre/post-test experiment.

Many businesses and organizations specialize in these types of tests. Listed below is a small sample of companies that can help in your assessment. If you do not want to outsource the project, the last section of this chapter shows you how to design research studies that will allow you to do it yourself.

The following companies, which were covered in detail earlier, offer syndicated media and market data and offer services for creating customized data for a client. Because of the time and expense involved in collecting and analyzing these data, the rates these syndicated research companies charge may appear high, however, as the saying goes "data are cheap, information is expensive." It is best for individual entrepreneurs to explore each of these sources to find out which types of data and information may be the best fit for their advertising executions and campaign:

- Gallup Polls
- Starch Readership Report (Starch INRA Hooper)
- Nielsen Media Research
- A.C. Nielsen
- Mediamark Research, Inc. (MRI)
- Information Resources, Inc. (IRI)
- ASI Market Research, Inc.
- Arbitron
- Simmons Market Research Bureau (SMRB)
- Standard Rate and Data Service (SRDS), especially the publication *Lifestyle*
- Sales and Marketing Management's *Survey of Buying Power.*

Keep in mind that this is a small list. There are many more organizations and businesses that can help you in this endeavor. We also recommend attempting to get some assistance from your local colleges and universities.

Often, there may be a small business development center located in your market area. Your local small business development center, or SBDC, is a subdivision of the United States Small Business Administration (SBA) and will have oceans of resources for you. Typically, an SBDC will also have trained consultants available to help with specific problems at prices greatly lower than their commercial counterparts. Use them. Also, approach professors who specialize in the types of evaluation you would like to undertake. Besides business professors, you may have some additional luck with public relations, communication design, electronic media, geography (for GIS evaluation and research), psychology, and sociology professors.

When you begin your evaluation process, the following general areas will have the biggest impact in terms of helping you learn what you did well and not so well:

- Sales data (including industry averages as well as your own data)
- Sales inquiries. Part of the IMC process is to create an interest in your target market for your products and services. Inquiries help to understand that interest, need, or want for your product(s).
- Attitudes, awareness, and likeability
- Recognition
- Recall

Evaluation, unfortunately, is the keystone of any great advertising or IMC plan. Having said that, evaluation is also one of the areas most often ignored by entrepreneurs because of its somewhat complex nature. Measurement and evaluation must involve much more than just checking sales data, counting returns on promotions such as coupons, or measuring the value of a public relations execution (where the value is oftentimes super inflated). The point is that there must be a grounded, ongoing analysis of a campaign's effectiveness, or else we are all doomed to fail in our future advertising and marketing communications.

DO-IT-YOURSELF: SETTING UP AN ADVERTISING
OR MARKETING RESEARCH STUDY

As stated earlier, many entrepreneurs (by their very nature) prefer to undertake the research, measurement, and evaluation process themselves. Most of the time, these self-evaluations are weak because no particular system was used, incorrect metrics were used, the sampling theory was faulty, or the sampling process itself was weak or flawed. There are very specific rules that must be followed when it comes to undertaking your own measurement and evaluation. This section provides a basic framework for marketing research (or other business research). This framework should be adapted and modified for the development of a particular, specific research undertaking.

An Overview and Steps

Daily, entrepreneurs call us asking for help in undertaking research programs. As such, we typically ask them to prepare a research proposal identifying everything they want to accomplish and the work that they already performed. If they have already undertaken an initial situational analysis, it makes the research collection job a lot easier. Additionally, some entrepreneurs may want to send out requests for proposals from professionals. A request for proposals (RFPs) must be developed based upon the type of information the business owner would like returned. In other words, the proposal plays the part of the outline for your research undertaking. Because of the abundant use of proposals in business, and in particularly in advertising and marketing, we have developed an overview of the stages one needs to go through to develop and understand the research proposal process.

Typically in any research undertaking, a proposal is developed to make sure that all variables and processes for the research are included. Usually you will want to take the following steps:

1. Read all that you can on the subject in the library or on credible Web sites.
2. Write down the decisions or outcomes you desire.
3. Research objectives (detailed). What is it, specifically, that you wish to understand? What are your informational needs?
4. What budget do you plan to have available for your research?
5. How are you going to collect the information you need? (Phone calls, postal mailings with a fax-back number, and focus groups are a few choices.)
6. Where will you store the information? In paper files? In a spreadsheet or database program? In a statistical analysis package program like SPSS or SAS?
7. What will you use to collect your data: questionnaire, observational recording sheet, something else?
8. Who will you collect the data from? (your sampling methodology)
9. How will you analyze the data? Just by looking at it? Statistically?

Let's take a look at each of these areas individually:

The first step is to undertake a situational analysis for the research study. You need to review all of the literature that is available to you that gets to your problem. This process is called a *literature review*. You need to have a great understanding of the market in which you are researching prior to initiating your research study. Additionally, while you are out searching already completed studies and information, you may run into some information that solves your problem, thereby erasing the need for you to perform additional research. These are time and money saving discoveries. If there are no outside studies that have been undertaken to solve your problem and answer your questions, are there studies that are close to the one you are undertaking that will provide you with some guidance on what to look or how to develop your methodology? Are there studies that have metrics that you can use? Are there studies that you can emulate in terms of undertaking your sampling? Gather all possible secondary data (data that have already been generated and collected) to see if there are some common themes in the studies. You will find that secondary data often solve your problems and allow you to forgo the tedious task of conducting your own primary research.

Concurrently with your review of the literature, you need to undertake a thorough review of your current situation. The situational analysis from your marketing plan will simplify this step. Some of the information and data you will want to look for will include information about your customer markets (e.g., What market segments provide the greatest advertising opportunities? What customers should be targeted for our audience? How are we going to position our brand in that particular market group?). Also, provide information on your company itself (this will help others to see how you see your business versus how others, including your customers, see it). Provide data on your customer base and your competitors. Without a clear picture of the market, your research will be doomed to failure.

Review the outcomes or decisions you desire. As stated earlier, you must have a specific outcome in mind when undertaking research. Research projects will answer one question at a time, and often will create additional questions that will have to be answered. The better you individuate your problem statement, the more valid your research findings will be.

In order to measure anything, there must be a benchmark or metric to measure against. *Research objectives* provide this benchmark. Thus, at the beginning of your research you need to think about what, specifically, you hope to accomplish. In writing your research objectives, keep in mind the following: (1) Make sure the objectives are time-bound. In other words, make sure there is a "due date," (2) Make sure your objectives can be measured against a metric or base, (3) Make sure the information is needed and cannot be generated through your review of the literature.

Your data collection system must be developed. In this step, you must identify your data sources (i.e., Where will your data be coming from? Who should be sampled?). Second, it is necessary to identify the method you will use to collect the data. This may be via questionnaire, phone interview, personal interviews, focus groups, observation, or other methods. In other words, how will you accumulate all of the data and information you will need to make an accurate assessment and evaluation of your executions? Remember there are two types of data: secondary data (which has already been collected for a different reason, but may still apply to your situation and offer a solution), and primary data (information collected for your specific purpose or to solve your problem). The two basic methods of collecting primary data are observing and asking.

Once you have your research design, you need to create, or develop, an instrument or to collect the data. This form will be used with primary data collection, but is not needed for secondary research. Most often, the data collection instrument used is a questionnaire. As such, you must create an accurate, valid, and reliable questionnaire that addresses the informational needs you have.

- You will need a sample of your current or future customers, therefore you need to develop a sampling plan that addresses:
- The population you are interested in studying.
- The sampling frame (this is simply a list of all items or people in your population. It could be phonebook).
- The sample selection process that you will use when selecting the sample.
- The sample size necessary to employ a statistical analysis of your data.

After you have the basic sampling plan in mind, you need to collect those data and then process them. There are several techniques used in this step. We recommend that you use a statistical program, such as SPSS or SAS to help with this task. Hand analysis is time-consuming and typically creates more errors than using a mechanical method of analysis. This step requires that you record your raw data which, in the next step, are turned into useful information.

Analyze and interpret your data. When you undertake the data analysis, you will find that the results can range from very sophisticated to fairly simple (i.e., using means, medians, modes, percentages, percentiles, quintiles, standard deviations, etc.). We recommend the more sophisticated techniques that allow for multivariate comparisons.

Document your findings and present them to all of the stakeholders in the advertising process, such as your agency, media buyers, your personnel involved in your advertising, consultants, and others to whom you are looking for help. It is useless to undertake this research if you are not going to use the results.

Sometimes research is a difficult process to understand and use, but with practice you will get better and better. Also, keep in mind that there are firms and individuals (consultants) who specialize in this type of work. If the price is right, we recommend that you outsource this work in order to generate more time for you to spend on day-to-day operations. This is *not* a step or task that you can afford to skip or do on the cheap. The results will drive your advertising and make you much more effective in reaching your targeted audience. This, in turn, will drive additional people to your business and result in a healthier bottom line.

WHAT WE HAVE LOOKED AT

In this chapter, we examined how to put the advertising plan together and measure its effectiveness. Specifically, we considered:

- The concept of evaluation
- The issue of doing it yourself versus outsourcing the work

- What, specifically, needs to be evaluated
- Steps in the do-it-yourself method

You are now ready to create your own advertising. We wish you good luck. In the final chapter, we will take a look at some trends and issues that will persist or occur over the next 5 to 10 years. Having an understanding of the environment in which you are working will also help you to create a better advertising program.

SUMMARY

☑ During your evaluation process, refer back to your goals and objectives to determine which you have met and which you have not.

☑ Always record your evaluation measurements in a way that will give you a gauge by which you can compare future evaluation efforts and help to set new goals and objectives moving forward.

☑ Many consumers do not mind being part of a company's research, as long as you are up-front, professional, nonintrusive, concise, and possibly offer them some form of incentive for participation.

☑ Use the information and data you have collected to your advantage.

10

The Future for Entrepreneurial Advertising

The field of advertising is impacted by changes more than most other areas of business. Technological changes have resulted in the development of new message media, such as the Internet, that allow advertisers to reach their targeted audiences better and with more targeted messages. Changes in social behavior, such as the use of online social networking sites (Facebook, Twitter, etc.), has made advertising research and executions much more effective in terms of targeting the market, however advertisers are also charged with the development of best practices that allow them to utilize these new opportunities effectively. Because "the only constant in the universe is change," entrepreneurs need to develop a system for assessing their advertising environments.

ENVIRONMENTAL SCANNING

In order to keep up with the changes in the advertising world, we recommend that you develop your own system for *environmental scanning*. Environmental scanning refers to reviewing the environments that impact your business, such as the technological environment, the legal environment, the natural environment, the social environment, and so on. For example, green marketing has become a big issue within the natural environment, and text messaging and cell phone use have impacted the social environment, especially for younger consumers, in a big way. If you know which environments impact you, your job will be easier and your advertising will be more effective. Environmental scanning allows you to prepare strategic responses to those changes and is very proactive.

Environmental scanning is relatively easy to undertake; success is dependant upon the entrepreneur's ability to predict the changes and react to those changes in a positive, strategic manner, as the whole concept of environmental scanning calls for individual entrepreneurs to adapt to change. In order for this to occur, there must be continuous input from all individuals, and flexibility in terms of communication. These traits are ones that entrepreneurs generally have, thus the job gets a little easier.

One example of how companies scan the environment to predict change can be seen with the Sherwin-Williams Company. Sherwin-Williams uses two basic retail divisions to service their customer base. While one of Sherwin-Williams' customer bases was in the do it yourself (or DIY) market category, the other retail division was in the contractor market category. Sherwin-Williams has been selling paint and paint accessories for over 150 years. When they hired Bob Wells to serve as their new IMC Director, they found out that some of their conventional thinking of the past was incorrect. The market for Sherwin-Williams had always focused on the contractor. In fact, when Sherwin-Williams made changes to their merchandise mix and their retail stores, in was typically in response to what the contractor market was telling them. The data and information that Sherwin-Williams generated from contractors was found to be correct for that portion of the market. However, when they looked at the DIY market, they were in for a surprise. Sherwin-Williams had always thought that their DIY market was made up of men. After all, Sherwin-Williams had been servicing these types of buyers (men) for over 150 years. After Wells join company, he undertook an environmental scan of his customer and market bases and was surprised to learn that the DIY division Sherwin-Williams had identified had been selling and marketing to the wrong targeted market. It was, in fact, women who made almost all of the decisions when it came to paint in the DIY market. Because of their diligence in undertaking an environmental scan, Sherwin-Williams was able to make the necessary corrections to their advertising and marketing communications. They no longer sell paint; they now sell home decorating ideas: "Ask How, Ask Now, Ask Sherwin-Williams." Additionally, to go with their IMC program, Sherwin-Williams no longer calls their retail personnel "sales professionals," but rather they refer to them as "home decorating specialists." Sales are up and everything is back to normal at America's largest paint (and home decorating) manufacturer and retailer.

In environmental scanning, we are looking for changes in the environment that have a potential impact on advertising and IMC programs. The economy is one of those that needs to be monitored. The first step is to define which environments will affect your business. The advertising environment is generally uncontrollable, thus entrepreneurs must adjust to environmental changes. It is important that entrepreneurs only select those environments that may have an impact on their business. The reason for this is that there are too many environments to scan, and the costs, both capital and human, can become quite high when undertaking the scanning process. Consequentially, smart entrepreneurs make sure they know what market they are operating in, and which environments will have an impact on that market. Some of the environments that entrepreneurs should pay heed to include:

- The social environment
- The technological environment
- The economic environment
- The governmental and legal environments

- The natural environment
- The competitive environment
- Any other environment that may have an impact on your business operations.

Since we are looking at environmental forces that are external to our business, it is essential that we include all relevant environments. We must look for outside forces and their relationship to the business, as well as their effects and potential effects on our organization. Environmental scanning is the process that seeks information about events and relationships in an organization's outside environment and the knowledge that assists entrepreneurs in running organizations or companies and establishing a mission, vision, goals, and objectives.

Scanning involves the collection of information and the analysis of outside forces. Entrepreneurs must avail themselves of all information that is available in regard to the markets. After identifying the markets, they need to pay due diligence to the environment as it very well may impact the business's operations. Additionally, you will need to collect information and analyze it as it applies to events, relationships, and crisis avoidance or a better understanding of the social, technological, governmental, natural, political, legal, economic, and other environments in your community. The responsibility for this undertaking should be a line management function, if not performed by the entrepreneurs themselves.

Below are the some basic steps that are required for successful environmental scanning:

1. Identify and current or potential changes that are occurring. These changes should have an impact on your business.
2. Monitor these changes. The direction of the change, the nature of the change, the force of the change, and the rate of change are all important aspects.
3. Forecast the probability that these changes (or that the change) will occur. What will be the impact on your business? What is the timing? What are some of the potential consequences you will face as a result of this change occurring?
4. Develop and implement strategic responses.

While performing your scanning function, focus on probabilities, the consequences, and the timing. Additionally, stay flexible. You may need to develop counter-forces and strategic responses.

To further generate data for your environmental scanning, we suggest you think about the following:

- Who do we monitor? Which groups, individuals, organizations?
- What do we monitor or forecast? What are the activities and processes used that are causing this change?
- Identify, as specifically as possible, the relevant change.

- Interpret the change as an environmental force (i.e., What is currently occurring in government? Technology? Society? How will this impact and affect me?).
- Provide an actionable response to the change that limits its impact on your business or organization. Be proactive.

We all know the stories of Ford's Pinto. We also know the story of the Tylenol scare. We want to refresh your memory and use these stories as examples of successful and not so successful environmental scanning programs. When the over-the-counter drug Tylenol became available to consumers, the makers of Tylenol knew that there was the potential for its abuse. Company personnel tried to brainstorm all of the situations that could potentially occur. While they had thought about overdoses, they had not thought too much about poisoning until one of the workers read an article that detailed what could happen if someone were to poison some of America's favorite products. With this information in hand, Tylenol developed a strategic response for use in case this ever happened. As you likely know, it did. The day after someone snuck into a number of stores and laced the pills with poison, the company's president was on television telling all who would listen what a tragedy that was. In addition, he mentioned the strategic plan that Tylenol had already put in place. He told America that the company would no longer manufacture capsules, but rather would begin the immediate production of caplets, which are much harder to tamper with. Furthermore, they would put the caplets in a blister package, which would be placed in a box with a seal. The box with the seal would then be shrink-wrapped to deter people from tampering with the product. In addition to changes in the product's safety and packaging, Tylenol was prepared to provide help to the families of those who had died. After initial slumping sales, Tylenol actually increased their sales to pre-crisis levels and then increased them more to generate record sales of the product. This was quite a positive outcome from such a terrible situation!

In the case of the Ford Motor Company, all transportation companies realize that there can be safety concerns surrounding the products they sell. Ford found this out when they began selling the Pinto. When certain Pintos were hit from behind, they had the potential to explode. This happened on a few occasions, killing and seriously injuring passengers. Ford undertakes environmental scanning, but found this situation to be a normal one. Ford believed that the consumers of its products would already know the dangers involved in driving an automobile, but this belief was incorrect. Ford did not take responsibility for any of the incidents, and instead took a seemingly uncaring stance. The company announced that people should know this type of thing could happen, and they offered to fix the cars through an international recall of the model. The social environment did not like this strategic response. The public was so outraged by Ford's response that they quit buying the Pinto (and some of Ford's other products) in protest. As a result, Ford quit making the Pinto due to a lack of market demand. It is indeed important to understand your market and the changes that continually occur within it.

With a basic knowledge of environmental scanning, we have the ability to scan our business environments to help predict what trends will occur, what changes to our business models we will have to make, and what potential traps lie head for us as we continue to operate.

POTENTIAL CHANGES IN THE ADVERTISING ENVIRONMENT AND LANDSCAPE

This section looks at some potential changes that are occurring, or may occur, in the advertising industry. In today's environment, from an advertising professional's viewpoint, technology and the economy will lead the way in terms of creating change. With the tremendous technological changes and the U.S. and world economies going into recession (and possibly depression in some areas), advertisers will have to create value with less capital and human resources.

In terms of technology, let's take a look at some of the things that will impact our advertising operations during the next few years.

The move to video and high definition (HD). By 2009, HD penetration into the marketplace had reached 34 percent of all U.S. homes. This figure is expected to reach over 50 percent by 2010 and even larger percentages by the end of 2011. As such, advertisers must readjust their production of commercials so that they are in HD, or are at least HD compatible. This will increase the costs associated with advertising production and pursuing broadcast and cybermarketing advertising.

Advances in the quality and speed of on-line advertising will also be associated with changes in technology. Many companies are experimenting with technology that will compete in the rich media arena (currently Flash is the market leader). Along with these advances, we feel that real time media flow protocol (RTMFP) will allow for better advertising online.

Advertisers will continue to crowdsource. Instead of outsourcing social research, companies will embrace crowdsourcing. Crowdsourcing lets the advertiser or corporate entity identify social networks where individuals are interacting with each other and research these "conversations" on the social networking sites. Hints are often provided during these conversations (such as the "coolest actor in TV today") that help advertisers create better and more effective "consumer-focused" messages. Prior to being able to achieve effective crowdsourcing data, advertisers had to "outsource" this function to other professionals who were already tied in to physical social networks. Trend spotters are using social networking extensively as they attempt to identify and label the next trend. This will dominate advertising's social media research.

There will be an increase in mobile advertising because of the giant gains mobile media continues to see in the marketplace.

Twitter will be used to develop brands and will drive brand revenue.

Networking will gain in popularity as advertisers discover the value of promoting and generating research via online social networking. In particular, Facebook, along with LinkedIn, Twitter, Xing, and Xanga, will lead this charge.

National cinema advertising will revert to local advertisers as national advertisers (with the exception of the government) opt for other media.

In addition to the technological gains, our environmental scanning also suggests that the following trends may also develop or continue into the 2020s:

Businesses (and in particular IMC and advertising specialists) will begin to launch new advertising campaigns internally so as to generate employee buy in to campaigns prior to their external launches. Employee excitement will drive the brand and keep the marketers focused on the important aspects of the campaigns.

There will be changes in the ethnic and race demographics. For example those with Hispanic ethnicity are in the fastest growing ethic demographic in the United States. People are aging (think baby boomers). As America ages, consumers will want and need new and different products. Advertisers will have to adapt to those changes.

Advertising and IMC research will once again gain importance. Over the past 10 years, advertisers have foregone a lot of quantitative research to concentrate on qualitative research. Since qualitative research should not be quantified (i.e., turned into numbers), hard, quantitative research studies will emerge.

Print media will continue to struggle as consumers go online to get their news and information. Additionally, television news stations will also suffer viewer loss, but will gain loyal viewers, enabling them to offer advertisers the ability to target within newscasts based upon the viewers' demographics.

As we continue to move toward globalization, advertisers will have to develop more than one campaign for each brand. The need to integrate all marketing communications will become important. Developing nations will utilize mass marketing while developed nations will have to be segmented as their consumer bases become increasingly heterogeneous.

Retailers and other businesses that have a research-based, comprehensive IMC and advertising program will expand and concentrate on brand development. Many companies have planned expansions based upon the current poor economy. These include AT&T Mobility, Au Bon Pain, Best Buy, CVS, Costco, Panera Bread Company, Five Guys Burgers and Fries, Forever 21, Noodles and Company, and Gold's Gym. These companies have focused on customer satisfaction and service, thereby building their brands' reputation. These companies will use nontraditional media coupled with some spending in traditional media in order to expand. They will have a good footprint in the future market.

Point-of-sale advertising and promotion will continue to grow as the point-of-purchase industry discovers new metrics for measuring advertising effectiveness at the point of purchase. This trend will also be seen in the online retail environment, where retailers try to generate additional sales and impulse buys by creating point-of-purchase displays in cyberspace.

Sports advertisers will continue their spending, but with a decrease in the total amounts spent. There are many cutting edge advertising methods available for new advertising placements. For example, Turner Sports has developed a method to allow advertising sponsors to appear on the television (or computer/mobile) screen without interrupting any of the regularly scheduled sports events. This adds additional time for sale by cable, network and independent television stations.

Digital signage will continue to grow. This also offers the media additional methods to grow advertising revenues. Digital signs appear to capture the attention of drivers and other consumers more effectively than traditional outdoor signage.

Buzz Marketing Will Continue to Grow

Guerrilla marketing will increase as advertisers look for ways to generate efficiencies as well as continue to generate reach.

The use of multi-platform campaigns will continue to be used to reach the marketplace with a consistent message. IMC will become increasingly more popular with businesses and nonprofit organizations.

Entrepreneurs must use the knowledge they gain from scanning various environments to take advantage of the changes that are occurring. Begin to advertise where your consumers are. Take advantage of social networking sites. Build change into your advertising and IMC plans. Prepare strategic responses to any and all events that you feel could impact your business. Continue to scan the environment for changes. Those who find the changes first and adapt their plans to them will be the companies and organizations that will be around for years to come.

Listed above are just a few of the environments we advertisers need to keep our eyes on. Remember, the only constant in the universe is change, and the more we monitor that change, the more effective and integrated our advertising can become.

RECAP

This final chapter discussed:

- Environments in advertising
- The system of environmental scanning
- Changes in the environment of which we need to be aware
- Future expectations within the world of advertising and some examples of companies that have begun to identify these changes and adapt accordingly.

SUMMARY

☑ Advertising is an ever-changing arena.
☑ Do not overlook the potential for marketing within emerging technologies and through online entities such as social networking sites, but be aware that

your customer can quickly tell when you are attempting to be something you are not.

☑ Always assess your advertising environments. Your success as an entrepreneur is dependant upon your ability to predict the changes and react to them in a positive, strategic manner.

☑ As an entrepreneur, your ability to adapt to environmental changes is likely greater than the average business owner.

☑ Learn from the mistakes of others.

☑ Do not be afraid to blaze your own trail.

☑ Keep a close eye on nontraditional media, as it will be used more and more to cut through the clutter of busy mass-media messages.

☑ Focusing on customer satisfaction and service is *never* a bad idea.

A FEW FINAL THOUGHTS

As we pointed out in the first chapter of this book, advertising is a complicated but necessary function for all businesses and organizations. It is essential for any start-up business or any business that operates with an entrepreneurial spirit. The first chapter introduced you to the wacky world of advertising. In following chapters, we spoke to you about how to create effective entrepreneurial advertising. Chapter 9 brought all of the concepts together, and chapter 10 made predictions for what the next few years will look like in the advertising industry.

We hope that you will be able to use this book to create a stronger brand and drive business to your organization. Should you require assistance during this process, please feel free to contact either of us with your questions.

We thank you for your purchase of this book and wish you continued success with all of your professional and personal undertakings. Should you wish to explore additional methods for the creation of a more effective business, please check out the other books in this series developed with entrepreneurs' needs in mind.

Index

About the Authors

JAMES R. (DOC) OGDEN has been described by communication design specialist Leslie Klopp as a "modern Renaissance Man." Dr. Ogden is well-known in the integrated marketing communications and advertising industries, having consulted with numerous national, regional, and international companies and organizations. Doc is a much sought-after public speaker, and, as such, has limited his speaking appearances to just four per year. In addition to one-on-one consulting, Doc has spoken to groups as small as one and as large as 1,000. He continues to lecture all over the world, and has made over 100 appearances in the Caribbean, the Bahamas, Central, North and South America, Asia, and Europe. Dr. Ogden has published over 60 research-based articles and is the author of six books on marketing, advertising, and business.

In his spare time Dr. Ogden keeps busy with his hypnosis practice (he is a certified hypnotherapist), music (percussion and guitar), reading, working in the entertainment industry (Doc recently was a featured actor in the movie *The Wicked One*), and spending time with his family.

SCOTT RARICK is a successful advertising executive. Mr. Rarick is connected to numerous organizations, such as the American Marketing Association (AMA), the American Advertising Federation (AAF), and Sales and Marketing Executives International (SMEI). Scott maintains an active membership with his local AAF chapter and regional ad club, and he frequently speaks at colleges and universities in the eastern United States. Scott's roles at his advertising agency, The Stevenson Group, include Director of Media and Director of Account Services, and his greatest strengths lie in brand management and development and strategic planning, strategic media implementation, and creative execution. Scott is the 2009 recipient of the Lehigh Valley SUITS "Turning the Curve" Award, sponsored by the United Way of the Lehigh Valley for his work involving nonprofit organizations. Prior to joining his current firm, Scott worked for numerous agencies within the Philadelphia DMA. Scott has serviced both B2B and B2C accounts over his career, and his clients have ranged from global industrial manufacturers to regional financial and health care institutions. Scott is an Eagle Scout, and hopes that his two sons follow in his footsteps.